for Tom & Carol
Enjoy!
Bill Alcorn
1-31-10

My Affair with S

48 Personal Essays, including a
special section on Noetic Science
(Consciousness, Intuition, and Spirituality)

Bill Alcorn

ISBN: 1-4392-6884-3
ISBN-13: 9781439268841

CONTENTS

INTRODUCTION

The 48 pieces assembled in this book are personal essays for family, friends and other readers. They include about half my creative writing output from 1998 to 2009 not counting play scripts. Personal means the author appears in them, from memoirs (as a main character) to essays of ideas (as a commentator). Anne Fadiman has suggested the term "familiar essay" to characterize her engaging essays halfway between the two extremes of heart and head. I have a few of those, too.

All the pieces started life in a non-fiction writing group organized by the Case Western Reserve University Continuing Education Department. A writing group is essential for those of us who need to collect our thoughts in words but don't have an external timetable. We often remark that writing requires three things: something to say, some ability to write, and a deadline. The group provides that important deadline. It also provides an atmosphere of good friendship and a wide variety of subjects and writing styles. So my first acknowledgment is to my fellow writers and our facilitator, Linda Tuthill, for their warm support and constructive feedback.

I have one special interest, the evolving field of consciousness studies, sometimes called noetic science; these essays are grouped under "Science, Consciousness, and Spirituality." The title essay "My Affair with S" (1998) leads off this section. I've tried to minimize the overlap in ideas and examples to the extent that one piece, "A Very Brief Tour of the Nonphysical Universe", has references to other essays rather than repeated material.

All the essays are arranged chronologically in five sections, mostly to remind me how my thinking has changed over time, especially in the Science section. A few of the pieces have evolved into lay sermons at my Unitarian-Universalist Church (two included) and presentations to a local philosophical group (three included). Two essays were published as guest op-ed columns in the *Cleveland Plain Dealer.*

The most important acknowledgment: my wife Susan, always my number one proofreader/editor. Susan also appears in "we" in several of the essays, as we have explored consciousness and other ideas together.

Contact me if you want to start a conversation at wralcorn@gmail.com. Put "Book" in the subject line.

Bill Alcorn
Cleveland Heights, OH
October, 2009

MEMOIRS and FAMILY

June, 1998
The Summer of 1985

I have a pretty good memory but I have trouble with the summer of 1985. I have to dig out old calendars to get the sequence of events right and even then most days are blank.

I do fine with 1953, when I entered college, taking the train myself from Chicago to Boston, so apprehensive about the changes ahead of me that I couldn't sleep. Or 1961, when I had an appointment to teach for a year in New Jersey on a week's notice, and we couldn't get the piano into the one-bedroom apartment.

1964 is easy. The first week of January we brought my new son home from the hospital on a crisp winter day with a blue sky, with such joy I could hardly imagine. We played the Mozart clarinet concerto on the hi-fi for him that first afternoon.

Even 1941 is surprisingly clear through a small boy's memory because of our move from an apartment to a house. Stopping at the neighborhood draft board office on Halloween with my parents and little sister, who was asleep behind her mask. Getting my own bedroom.

In 1992 I was able to help my son and his wife pay for a trip to a medical clinic that resolved a medical issue and resulted in my first grandson in 1993. It brought back 1964 all over again.

I also bought my first red car in 1992.

In the fall of 1986 I met Susan and I knew very quickly that we would marry, and we have argued ever since about who knew first.

In 1970 I drove very fast to the hospital early one June morning. Five minutes after we arrived, my daughter was born while I was parking the car. Another miracle. I called my son first.

In 1954 my mother died although I missed the last few weeks of her life, being away at school and being spared what my father and sister experienced. I know she would have liked to have me there but I cannot reconstruct what role I might have played. I'm grateful for being spared, except that I'm not very familiar with death.

I was also in my first hurricane in 1954.

In 1967 I was in the hospital when my father died, full of tubes, but I was not with him at that moment. I was probably having coffee or a cigarette or both. The day before, when he asked me if he were going to die, I didn't know what to say. Now I do, but 31 years have passed and it doesn't count for much.

I could certainly relate some important things about 1959 and 1968 (that was some year for all of us), and 1994, 1980 (too much turmoil and sadness to forget), 1950, and 1975 (my heart attack), and most of the rest of them. Except the summer of 1985.

Early in 1984 I was promoted to Director of a research department of about 40 people where I had been a group leader. I loved everything about the job despite the turmoil of yet another change of ownership of the company. Within a few months, the new owners decided to reorganize and install their own managers. To my surprise I was fired one day early in 1985.

I was in a two year marriage to a hard working woman who had returned to grad school. I was also supporting my son in college, and there were no other positions for my specialty in the region. The marriage ended in the spring, soon after I started looking at jobs elsewhere in the country.

I managed to keep my son in college with extended credit cards, and for the second time in my career I was unemployed. Only this time I was draining my financial resources at an alarming rate. All I could think of every day was finding job openings, preparing and mailing resumes, waiting for the mailman, and calling friends and contacts until they slowed down returning my calls.

Corporate upheavals are commonplace today and, for the most part, I knew what to expect in the job market. However, I did not expect that I would drop most of the activities I had enjoyed for years. Not because of cost or time required, but because I simply lost interest.

I barely read the daily paper except for the employment section. I stopped reading the many magazines I received and let the subscriptions expire. I stopped playing or listening to music. My social life was minimal. My close friends often took the initiative in getting me out somewhere. It was job, job, and job in that order. Even my friends got tired of hearing about the great job search.

I don't think depression is the right word for my state at that time. Dullness, maybe. A lack of excitement or feeling of growth or movement, or participating in significant events, or experiencing joy, even small joys.

The peculiar thing about joy is that there is always some around to experience, as I understood later. Humor's a joy, as is a smile or a good night's sleep, or a well written paragraph, or a shoeshine, or a thousand other things of everyday life.

So maybe what I'm talking about is being unaware of life all around me. Living in the past or in the future. Not being present.

I wasn't present in the summer of 1985. That's why my calendar is blank.

February, 1999

It Wasn't Even Close

My elementary education in the 40's was in the Kenwood School, part of the Chicago Public Schools. The superintendent was Robert Maynard Hutchins, formerly President of the University of Chicago and a major figure in American public education.

Kenwood was a special example of an urban integrated school. It served a neighborhood about equally divided among Catholics, Protestants, and Jews, and to a small but growing extent, was racially integrated. Some of the Jewish families were refugees who had made it out of Germany before the war. It certainly had a special flavor that was evident even to elementary students.

I remember the classrooms vividly. Every room had posters showing children of various colors and religions hand-in-hand.

My church, low-church Episcopal, was more progressive than most. The youth leader after the war was Father Mike, an American-born Japanese. We kids knew that was unusual, and we rather liked it as if we were part of some kind of post-war reconciliation.

The third part of my social orientation came in the YMCA groups for boys. These were totally integrated; the young men who supervised us were graduate students from a nearby YMCA college.

I would sum up the prevalent social values as supporting cooperation and understanding among the various religious, racial, and economic elements of our neighborhood. The common ground was the public school. The progressive culture was so regular, so routine, that I can't remember it ever being an issue among the kids.

I only discovered much later that most people I know did not pass through such a school system. Moreover, a growing number of Americans are very unhappy with the social values their children absorb in public schools. The largest group appears to be from the fundamentalist side of Protestant Christianity, and their solution is to support the Christian school movement, at considerable personal expense.

I understand their concern although I don't share it. In fact, the American public schools have been a very bright spot in our country's history. The schools and the civilian-run military (in particular, the draft) strike me as the two principal institutions responsible for our unique sense of one country. Unfortunately, both are on a steep decline in this role.

Clearly, my daily life experiences were surrounded by an impressive array of progressive values from school, YMCA groups, and church. In fact, it was so strong that I can hardly remember what social values my parents held – except that they chose to live in that neighborhood.

It wasn't until seventh or eighth grade that I even suspected there might be a conflict, and my awakening was jarring. My YMCA group was having a dance, and I was required to invite a girl. This was more uncomfortable than desirable, as I was still three years away from developing a hormonal interest in girls. Nevertheless, I did invite Judy, who sat next to me and was the best student among the girls.

Since I needed someone to drive us, I told my parents about the dance. My father agreed to drive; no problem. It was my mother's reaction that I remember today, fifty years later. She was upset about Judy having a Jewish family name and she handled it awkwardly. When I finally understood what upset her, I felt sorry for her, for her wrongness. Only much later did I get some perspective on mother's upbringing in a community with pervasive anti-Semitic sentiments. They were probably as routine and accepted as the progressive values in my world. Mother died when I was 18, after a long decline of health. We never had an occasion to resolve that incident.

I think I found an excuse to cancel the invitation to placate my mother. I certainly cannot recall anything about Judy except that she was smart and had dark hair, so it was obviously not much of a relationship. The lasting memory is the difficult lesson about values.

That marked the beginning of a series of life lessons for me. It was time to grow up, whether I liked it or not. Within the year I had a significant one in my religious thinking, too. One Saturday morning in June, I was walking to confirmation class in my church, near the end of several weeks of classes, when quite suddenly I had a new, very troubling, idea. I realized that I didn't believe what I was being taught. It was very clear, very definite. After a few minutes, I continued walking to the church, finished the series, and received confirmation soon thereafter. I liked the ministers and people at the church, but the theology was not for me. Twenty years later I joined a liberal religious church.

So what about the role of my public school in the Judy incident? It was very large, indeed. Mother was no match for the school system. It wasn't even close.

February, 1999
To Jared on His 6th Birthday

Dear Jared:

You and I went to Mama Santa's for pizza on your sixth birthday last month, and we finished our visit with some cookies from Presti's bakery. These are two good places to know about. I wouldn't be surprised if they're still around some years from now when you see this birthday letter.

We both learned some things that evening. I found out that you are smart and curious about the heavier things of life, and have a nicely developing sense of humor about the lighter things. I already know that you are loyal to your younger brothers despite considerable provocation, and you've been happy to help take care of them when they were infants. That's an impressive list of things to be when you are six.

Like other young people, you have an enormous personal databank waiting to be filled with information. In an hour or so, we worked our way through the map of Italy on the placemats, starting with your inquiries into what a map is, what is meant by countries and cities and islands, and why many things in the restaurant were colored red, white, and green. We talked of other things too, and I wish I had been clearer about some of them. It's quite a responsibility to introduce brand new subjects to someone, to start his file on "islands", for instance.

I'm looking forward to future discussions very much, but some things about conversations with a grandson concern me.

One is the huge amount of information we accumulate compared with the time we will have to talk about it. Another is when to introduce certain subjects. Another very important one is how to explain, even warn you, that some things I might say are mostly factual, while others are opinions. I don't think that distinction can be made too early.

When I was young, I was encouraged to think for myself and I certainly want to pass that notion on. It has led to a very full life for me. However, I have to tell you that it's often uncomfortable, even lonely, to resist the warmth of authority and strike out on your own. It's especially irritating when you discover you are on the wrong path. Thinking for yourself has to go along with learning when to admit you're wrong. This is rough stuff.

So we'll spend a little time talking about how to think, and how to build some trust in your ability to think. At the same time, it will be important to talk about how to listen, too.

Of course, you have to get through a lot of factual stuff first, before we talk much about thinking and logic and listening and analyzing and synthesizing. The schools are good at that. Maybe where grandparents can be most helpful is to go light on the facts and instead, spend our limited time on how to handle facts. Thinking, analyzing, and so forth.

One of my favorite ways of handling facts is extrapolation. That means making good guesses when you don't have all the facts. Some time we'll talk about work, and I might suggest that you find an occupation that requires good guessing. A lot of people become afraid of guessing, as if there's something wrong with it. Maybe they got the wrong message in school. The only way to invent things and ideas is to guess a lot; the results can be very exciting.

The kind of guessing I'm talking about is closely related to intuition. Not many years ago, intuition was believed to be something some people had and others didn't. It was widely said that women were better at it than men. Yet, I think everyone has this ability and there are ways to improve it. For some reason, many men are reluctant to admit to being intuitive in our society. Now it's true, because of historical divisions in activities between men and women, that women probably had more intuitive understanding of relationships between people, while men did more inventing of things and ideas. That's changing now as men and women are doing the same kind of work, and we're beginning to see that intuition is widely used by everyone, although it goes by different names.

So I look forward to talking about guessing and intuition. I'm excited about bringing up some very new ideas about where intuition comes from, and how it works.

Whether or not you learn how to become a good guesser, you will come up against some difficult questions about right and wrong, where facts don't help much. For instance, how do you decide what to do when your intuition tells you to go one direction, and people around you tell you to go the other? A century ago, such questions came under the heading of "moral development", a term rarely used at this time. All too often, it meant some rather restrictive practices like making young people learn a list of rules under the heading of religion, or sending them off to boarding schools to be tamed like young horses. Maybe grandparents can help a bit here, by pointing out the many ways people have developed a moral sense. This is an area where learning how to listen and think at the same time can get you through nicely.

I see that we have lots to talk about. I know of some other good restaurants you might like.

Happy birthday, with love, from Grandpa Bill.

March, 1999

My Early Sex Education

Sorry if the title misled you, as this brief memoir will not measure up in contemporary terms. It would be close to the truth to say that up to 9 or 10 years old, my sex education was non-existent, as was the word "sex" in public discourse. Older kids gradually learned the meaning of publicly mentioned words like "crime of passion" or "wedlock", but that took some work.

It was partly the times, the early forties. My adult media exposure was limited to the daily paper, the radio, *Life Magazine*, and *The Saturday Evening Post*. We also had the *Ladies Home Journal* and the *Woman's Home Companion* in our house, and I suppose they might have been mildly educational had I looked into them – although I imagine that sexual issues were mostly confined to romance and euphemism. My media favorites were comic books, which were universally devoted to winning the war.

Sex, especially the sexual conduct of public figures, would not become a staple in the media for many more years. The few books with anything other than romantic fantasy (D.H. Lawrence or Henry Miller, for instance) were unobtainable through any channel available to a child. The only kids who knew about such things had access through their parents' collections. Maybe sexual material was around but I certainly didn't know about it, nor did my friends.

Woody Allen, who was born the same year as myself, got big laughs in his early monologues telling how he got educated by looking at the brassiere ads in the *Sunday New York Times*. But those came along a decade later.

Woody probably also got much of his early sex education as the rest of us from that era did, by looking through stacks of old *National Geographic's* in someone's attic. Every issue seemed to have some photographs of naked African, Australian, or South American natives going about the business of living. I've always suspected that the *National Geographic's* legendary success as a publication had as much to do with those naked natives as the quality of its photography.

Before the Geographics, my first memory of anything suggesting that there was something special about the differences between men and women occurred when I was five. Because of illness, I never attended kindergarten. One day that year I was in Milwaukee with my mother, visiting my grandmother. While there, we visited a kindergarten class so I could see what school was like. I think I was left there for a half day and I participated in the scheduled activities. I had already taught myself to read with the help of my mother, so the reading portion was boring. Then there was nap time, where we each got a small rug from a chest and lay down. The best activity, drawing, came after the naps.

I can't recall whether we were told what to draw or could choose our own subject, but I set to drawing a man and a woman. I do remember trying to do a very careful job, because this was my first class ever. So I drew naked figures with breasts on the woman and genitals on both. Very carefully. When the time was up, the teacher came over. I was hoping for some praise for my careful work, but she seemed flustered, although with good humor. I think she said the drawing was fine as she picked it up and put it away. When my mother and grandmother returned, they had a short conference with the teacher amidst more fluster and obvious laughter. The best I could get from them later was that my naked drawings were fine, but not usually done that way.

I have sympathy for the adults, for I presented them with a complex issue. What was wrong with my drawings? How do you explain societal customs to a child without being overly directive? I think they did the best they could. However, from then on I clothed the figures I drew. I suppose I'm the better for it.

October, 1999

Learning the Hard Way

For several months during my single period in the eighties, I spent time with C, a divorced woman a few years younger than myself. I was out of work and frustrated at being overqualified by my education for most of the advertised job openings that I pored through daily. I frequently wondered why I had specialized myself into such an employment corner. C gave me some perspective on my situation through her own example.

She had lived with severe ADD – Attention Deficit Disorder – her whole life. Through her teenage years she had never been able to finish a book. She frequently had brown-outs as a teen, almost fainting at times. Around that time, it was discovered that she had a serious sugar imbalance (hypoglycemia) and through changing diet and some medication she reduced the severity of the condition. However, she was still ADD.

She somehow managed to finish high school and enroll in a state university, where she studied psychology and special education, and partially completed doctoral studies in education. Her specialty became teaching other people with ADD how to get through life.

I met her many years later and was attracted by her lively intelligence and positive nature. However, she had an unusual conversational style. I would say something to her, and she would say it back to me before responding. It was as if she had a time-delay tape in her brain, and needed to operate a few seconds out of real time. This was one of the skills she taught.

With C in mind, I became aware of the widespread incidence of ADD, Dyslexia, and related conditions among people who are smart and capable by any reasonable standards. They tend to cover up their particular problems of brain functioning and often cannot really name them. They often do poorly in academic subjects and find that the jobs available to them are well below their intrinsic skill levels. Consequently, many carve out independent lives where nobody points out daily, by word or other disparagement, that they can't write easily or don't seem to listen well.

I went to work for one such person not long after knowing C, a high-energy entrepreneur who had started a small technical company. He was uncomfortable with detailed planning or nearly any kind of meeting over 15 minutes, and he would jump on a plane to anywhere for what seemed like inconsequential reasons. He frequently displaced letters in his writing – which I was happy to correct when he gave me drafts to read. Yet, he had some outstanding personal qualities such as insight and empathy about people, and a willingness to trust others and to take risks. In earlier years I might have been critical of his shortcomings and less aware of his strengths, but my experience with C had given me better perspective.

There was a newspaper story a few years ago about a successful president of a financial firm who only realized he had ADD at age 46, when his daughter had similar problems. The process of discovery started with the girl's teacher who recommended an evaluation. He volunteered for the same tests and scored about the same as his daughter.

I don't know how I could have reached middle age and have had supervisory responsibility for dozens of people without being aware of these brain functioning conditions. I certainly never was exposed to any information on them in the many kinds of management training courses I had taken, in school, industry, or the military. I certainly was aware of the problems of the deaf and blind, but not of those challenged by ADD or dyslexia.

The school systems I attended were set up for people like me, with strong skills in word and symbol recognition (i.e., math), but average or below in things like musical pitch recognition and visual sensitivity. I still marvel at the ability of artist friends to see and work with small differences in color and texture. In music, I'm fairly good at sight reading and rhythm, but my pitch recognition is very weak. At one time, as an adult, I tried to learn to play jazz on an alto saxophone, but I just couldn't hear intervals that came easily to the better players – a skill essential to improvisation. I would often have a musical idea in my head, but I could not play it without trial and error. Like C, I would have to work it out with a "tape delay".

I played most sports that boys do, but was never very far from average. Yet I was a top student and accumulated more than my share of honors and good grades along the way. I have to conclude that in education as I experienced it, it's quite acceptable to be mediocre in music, art, and gym. It's not hard to guess the strengths of the people who set up school systems.

It would be good to explain these facts of life to young people. How we get different sets of genetic characteristics dealt to us just as we get born into different economic circumstances. That there is no right set, just different sets. That our job is to understand these differences and deal with them as necessary to cope in the world.

I remain very grateful to C for showing this to me, and especially for her personal interest in me at a time that I was unprotected by my educational accomplishments and status in the working world. It was nice to be with someone who looked past one's skills for the person behind them. I think I became better at doing that too.

February, 2000

On Cleaning My Files

Last summer I spent two weeks cleaning out my technical files, accumulated over 40 years. I threw out twelve cartons and kept two, probably unnecessarily. I carefully taped the discards so that my files and papers wouldn't spill all over the street, and lined them up on the curb as neatly as they had rested in my file cabinet, unused, for several years. It was the least I could do. The next morning I could not stop myself from watching the garbage truck take them away. It was one of those end-of-an-era moments you see at the end of movies just before the credits.

It needn't have taken two weeks at all. It could have been accomplished in two days. The additional ten days were taken up in reading through the files and remembering what I had done and the lessons I had learned in industrial research and development.

During nearly 40 years as a chemical engineer, I was a researcher and later a technical manager. The areas I worked in were the invention and testing of catalysts for chemical processes or the cleanup of environmental pollution; design of catalytic devices for vehicles and aircraft cabins; development of fuel cells and high-energy batteries; and some other odds and ends. This took place at four companies after graduate school.

Typical industrial catalysts are small pellets or powders through which flow liquids and gases, often at very high pressures or temperatures. The catalyst makes it possible for a desired chemical reaction to happen. The specialty I had studied in graduate work is the interaction of rates of flow and rates of reaction. This kind of information is the basis for designing reactors and processes.

I was fortunate to like what I did for a living, which was mostly to invent and test things, or to figure out how to make something work better or cheaper. In later years, I was involved in putting products and processes together to satisfy customers, and in helping other people learn to invent and test things. Since I was in industry, I did very little publishing of my results, although I have a few papers and patents. Satisfaction came in other ways.

The files stirred a few memories of my work life.

Gedunken experiments: One of my teachers spoke of "climbing down where the molecules are to understand how they behave." That appealed to me. I remember a few times when I gained insight into physical-chemical processes to the extent that I doubted anyone else in the world quite saw it my way. None of these insights brought about any revolutions in industrial practice, but some of them led to new or improved products that contributed profit to my employers.

The best memories are about those moments of insight and the feeling of uniqueness in the world. Uniqueness, not importance... it's a special feeling. It was not something I could explain very well to my wife or friends. You had to be there – down with the molecules. I found and saved a couple of those files.

Another peculiar pleasure I got from my work was predicting the outcome of experiments or field tests by mentally working through the experiment before doing it. In retrospect, this exercise had a significant intuitive component. At the time I thought it was just storing up and using experience. At one lab in the 70's, a few of us enjoyed an occasional Manhattan cocktail after work. We also got in the habit of betting on the results of experiments and tests, with Manhattans being the currency of bets. Results accumulated such that when I left the lab, I was 20 to 30 Manhattans ahead of second place.

Climbing down with the molecules or predicting experimental results were forms of "gedunken" experiments, worked through "in the head" before actually doing them. When you got good enough at this, you could often omit the physical experiment unless you needed confirmation data to sell the results to others.

Listening: In the late 60's I was in charge of a project to develop a rechargeable zinc-air battery for potential use in electric vehicles. (This idea emerged again at other companies in the 90's.) I had three PhD's and two or three technicians in the project, and we set up a room full of experimental battery cells being cycled 24 hours a day until they died out. This was quite an experienced team, but we were not making very good progress at one point.

We had the part-time assistance of a non-degree-holding mechanical design engineer named Dan to help us with hardware problems. Dan would come in early each morning, look around for any problems he would normally deal with, and then return to his area of the building. One day he came in and sat down, and asked about some peculiar jiggles on the voltage strip charts. The project group had accepted them as random static, but he persisted. When he finally got our attention, we found that the jiggles indicated a significant change in cell behavior. Dan had good eyes, and better, an inquiring mind. From that point on, he was involved in all project discussions.

Social change: In the 50's I worked at a paint manufacturing plant. We made varnish in large heated kettles, using what subsequently became a forbidden solvent, trichloroethylene. The workers in the vicinity were subjected daily to its fumes, which were not unpleasant to smell. If they got a large enough dose, the result was inebriation or a state of drunkenness. My company was fairly enlightened for the time. They allowed the drunken worker to lie down on a bench in the locker room while he sobered up, rather than sending him home and docking his pay for the hours lost.

At about the same time, a woman chemist applied for a laboratory job at the chemical company I later joined. She was required to walk back and forth in the view of her interviewers so they could check out her figure. She got the job, probably the first female professional at that location, and one of the first in the company.

In the same company, at about the same time, there was a simple procedure for getting rid of toxic waste. During the night shift, workers rolled drums of waste solvents down the hill to the nearby river and let nature take its course. The procedure was not recorded in any file, and the EPA was not yet even a concept. However, carrying it out on night shift indicated an early sensitivity to environmental concerns.

In the late seventies I hired a woman chemist from Israel, where women had occupied good professional positions for many years. She had excellent credentials and was very good at her work, justifying the high salary we offered. I soon found out that she was making 30% more than any other woman in the company, and this fact led to some unrest among the employees. Although she left after a short time for a job more suited to her experience, I think she also was influenced by the atmosphere.

One other recollection about social change. All the manufacturing plants in which I worked were racially integrated. Black men had lower level jobs than white men on the average, but more than a few held responsible positions as foremen or supervisors. I cannot remember any expressions of racial animosity at any of these places, rough as they were, particularly for women. On the contrary, the black workers were liked and respected by the white workers. I'm thinking of the period 10 to 30 years after the integration of the US Army in 1946 by President Truman, when racial prejudice was still widely prevalent in our society. (I hesitate to say "widely" now, as a comment on the social changes of the last 50 years.) I saw the same thing in the peacetime Army in the 50's. There is nothing quite like working together, and relying on each other in times of high activity and stress, to minimize racial barriers.

Men have always shared jokes in which some "other" ethnic group is the object of derision. In my experience, a significant exception is race jokes among men with either military or manufacturing experience.

Supervision: In industry, I started by doing individual projects, and worked my way up to supervising groups of professionals and technicians working in applied science, engineering, and technical sales. I could work with anyone who was primarily motivated to do a good job, whatever his/her ability or personal lifestyle. I did have trouble with those who had other primary agendas such as getting ahead as fast as possible or just getting through the day without falling asleep. Luckily, the good-job group was 90% of the people in my area of responsibility.

I looked at my job as setting the stage, arranging the environment, and clearing out the barriers so people could do their best, grow in the job, and contribute to the company. Within this mode of supervision, some conventions of the workplace were downgraded, and not infrequently I was in conflict with the rules.

Working hours, for instance. Recognizing that people had different daily work cycles, I pushed flex-time to its limits. Those who rose at 4:00 AM and were ready to work were allowed to come and leave early, some to tend to their small family farms. Others, typically single men, had very active evening social lives. It was unproductive to require them to be at their work stations at 8:00 AM, for they spent the first hour or two drinking coffee to wake up. They came late and worked into the evening, and often contributed in major ways. When someone had a pressing personal problem such as child care, we worked out a schedule that allowed him or her to take personal time as needed, in return for effective work at some other times.

In the 70's, my best technician, a true maverick, had a problem getting up in the morning. I remember calling him around 9:30 AM occasionally to wake him up. Then he would race to the lab, with his long hair, earrings, and obscene tee-shirts*, and accomplish more than anyone around him. Of course, I had to quietly adjust his personnel records from time to time.

* *Everybody's favorite tee-shirt was apparently from a construction company named the Richfield Erection Co. (Real or imaginary, I don't know.) It had a picture of a tall crane with the company slogan, "We always get it up."*

I came of age at a time when some bosses stood at the door at 8:00 AM, looking at their watches as the staff rushed to make it on time. Others would insist on clean desks at the end of the day, and would sweep anything left on a desk to the floor to emphasize the point. I also interviewed for a couple of jobs where I was told that work officially ended at 5:00, but we were expected to be there until at least 6:00 or 6:30. Somewhere I had picked up the notion that the key measure of people on the job was effectiveness, not duration, and I acted accordingly.

The file drawer space is now occupied by topics related to my current non-technical interests. But the imprint of those 40 years remains with me, even though the files are gone.

February, 2001
APB

In the fall of 1961, I was working in New Jersey near New York City. The previous year, I had taken up recorder playing and the study of early music with an enthusiasm that marks the adult amateur. Through LP records, I was acquainted with the handful of leading players of Renaissance and Baroque music, who were not as plentiful then as a few years later. When I discovered that Bernard Krainis was offering a series of evening group lessons in Manhattan on the art of ornamenting Baroque music, I signed up quickly.

Krainis was known as a virtuoso on the recorder through concerts and recordings. He also taught a growing group of New York wind players who wanted to add the recorder to their repertoire for commercial work.

Four or five of us, all amateurs, assembled in his West Side apartment, happy to spend a few hours with a Master. It was worth the effort of getting there, parking (!) and practicing, for Krainis treated us quite seriously. He set us to the two tasks of playing exercises with as much musicality as we could muster, and then to composing, and playing, our own embellishments in the late Baroque style.

I learned a few things about ornamentation, techniques that I used in later years in performance. However, the most important and lasting lesson had to do with playing routine exercises, the kind you would find in any method book for a musical instrument. Krainis insisted that we try to play them beautifully every time. He had us print "APB" at the top of every page of practice music, short for "Always Play Beautifully". It had nothing to do with skill level, but everything to do with attitude and focus.

I wrote APB on my practice music for many years after that, as I took up other wind instruments, and I think it helped make my limited practice time more effective and rewarding. At the time, I understood it to mean that one cannot expect to play beautifully in performance if you do not do so in practice. Some years later I realized that APB was a specific lesson derived from a broader truth, which might be stated like this: *Strive to function in all activities at a high level of attention to the matter at hand. You will like the results much better.*

What caused me to rethink APB was a workshop in "awareness" that Susan and I took a few years ago. We were taught to be aware, in any given moment, of all the messages that might be influencing us at that time: physical and emotional messages, outdated ideas, beliefs, fears, etc. If we could see all the possible messages pulling us one way or the other, we would be in the best possible state to behave appropriately. That doesn't mean we would always make great decisions or behave in an exemplary fashion, but we would be the best we could be, given the limitations of our knowledge, experience, and ability.

In the heightened emotional level of the workshops, it was probably easier to practice awareness. Yet it isn't very complicated. Not long after one of the sessions I was listening to a speaker who had just completed a lecture. He asked if there were any questions, and a few hands shot up, including mine. Just as my arm became fully extended, I became aware that I was intending to show off with my question, not gain knowledge. My hand came down as I reflected that I really had no interest nor need to show off at that time. Perhaps at any time.

It's not just emotions that interfere with behaving appropriately or playing beautifully. I'm a middle-of-the-pack amateur golfer. Everything seems to distract me from executing glorious golf swings, from sore muscles to noise, and particularly the memory of how badly I hit the ball on the last shot. So it's noteworthy that I played one of the best rounds of my life the week after we returned from one of the awareness workshops. Somehow, it was just me and the golf ball, the latter waiting to be hit in an appropriate arc for an appropriate distance. During that round, there were occasions when I actually played beautifully. I should consider putting "Always Swing Beautifully" on my golf card.

Focusing attention and staying aware of internal messages that are surrounding any activity will improve the results. A simple example might be cooking for friends, whether a simple breakfast or an elaborate recipe. It's not surprising that the best results occur when you focus on providing a pleasant dining experience. Showing off doesn't work as well.

Teaching is full of opportunities to teach beautifully. If you understand your job to be imparting a new idea to a student, you will look for the best way to do that. It's not always easy, but it is the mark of an aware teacher. I think that's what Krainis was about.

October, 2001
The Van Cliburn Piano Competition

One evening last week, after watching news of terrorists and anthrax, I came upon a PBS documentary of the Van Cliburn international piano competition. After ninety minutes and a series of strong emotional reactions, I turned off the TV after seeing the selection of winners. It had reached me in a much different way than the earlier reports of death and destruction.

The documentary was done very well. We saw pre-competition interviews of several contestants, their family members and coaches, and judges. We watched them pick out tuxedos and dresses to wear, confer with the orchestra conductor, and practice over and over and over. We listened to a handicapped contestant who carried a special piano bench with him, one who could not sleep at all the night before a competition, and a young Russian woman with a small child who played certain passages extremely softly. And performance excerpts from great piano works.

Why did I have such strong reactions? Was it the beautiful music, played well and intensely? Was it the struggle of competition? I've reflected on my own experiences as an amateur musician since my late twenties, particularly the earlier years when I was very active, and my first marriage to a professional singer. Perhaps the seeds are to be found there.

Janet and I were married from 1958 to 1980. In the first 13 years, she was a mezzo-soprano, then changed to dramatic soprano. This required a major shift in our repertoire. I say "our" because she practiced at home nearly every evening and weekend, so I became very familiar with her exercises and arias, such that I could sing along with her in my head. I knew the hard parts and would often stop what I was doing to listen to her work through them. I made small suggestions about phrasing or attacks or rests that were sometimes helpful. In the early years we lived in small apartments where I had little choice. Later, I could put two doors between the practicing and myself, but the music always got through the walls, like the smell of apple pie in a baker's home. When she changed repertoires, my musical memory bank did not adjust very well. I guess I will always remain a mezzo in my head.

Boston, 1964: I had started playing the oboe a year earlier with a second hand instrument and weekly lessons, and I had begun playing a bit with our early-music friends with whom I had played recorder for four years. However, I had never played any instrument in an orchestra or band. It was time. Being realistic about my progress, I asked several people for their opinion on the worst community orchestra in the area. The consensus was a town not far from Boston. So I called the conductor and asked if he could use someone to play last oboe. He was delighted, as he only had one oboist at the time. I showed up one fall evening with a pocketful of new reeds and a very sore lip; we started with a Mozart symphony they had been working on. The oboes sit right in the middle of the orchestra, and I took my place. We began, and I was so excited that I botched my first entrance. I had never really heard all those separate instruments before, when listening to concerts and records. I even heard the second violins and violas. I told my friends I had experienced polyphonic sound.

Provincetown, 1967: We attended an early-music week that summer, with New York faculty and a mixture of professional and amateur students. I was very excited to be in a small class of oboists taught by Robert Bloom from the New York Philharmonic. Most were serious students from the city. We spent the week sight-reading single lines from the keyboard scores of Bach's two and three part inventions. It was extremely frustrating for me, as I could not seem to play low notes, day after day. I made dozens of reeds and practiced until my lips were very sore, to no avail. I finally decided to drop out and spoke to Bloom. He took a look at my oboe, lit a cigarette, and blew smoke into the instrument. A wisp appeared next to one of the small trill keys through a very small crack. Apparently the wooden oboe did not like riding in our car trunk in the hot summer drive to Provincetown. I felt both relieved and stupid, and I was happy to return to my industrial research job where I had some confidence in what I was doing.

New York, 1968: After moving to Long Island, Janet sang some Gilbert and Sullivan operettas at New York City Center in the summer of 1967, and was invited to join the New York City Opera at their new home at Lincoln Center. She was still a mezzo-soprano, and was put to work understudying B and C roles (in an A-B-C rating system). In doing this, she had to learn the staging pretty much by herself, with few full rehearsals. Her first big break came when she was asked to sing the B role of Suzuki in Madame Butterfly at the last minute. It was an old production, so rehearsals were minimal. She got me a sixth row center seat for her debut. Although I had heard her sing for ten years, this was the big time, so I was very nervous (butterflies in *my* stomach?). It went very well, and I could relax a bit – until the flower duet. Butterfly and Suzuki are on stage, and there is quite a bit of stage business around the ringing of bells and a bouquet of flowers. At a critical point in the music, Butterfly throws the bouquet at Suzuki to catch. Unfortunately, Janet had her back turned and the flowers plopped onto the stage. She got through it fine, better than I did.

Long Island, 1969: I love the music of Bach and Mozart and Vivaldi... and Richard Rodgers. I had a chance to play oboe and English horn in the pit orchestra for a community production of "Oklahoma." Several of the great melodies in that show have solos for these instruments. It is exhilarating to play the inspired and intricate pieces of the masters of the 18th century, but it is just overwhelming to play the wonderful melodies of a modern master. To this day, I get emotional when attending a production of Rodgers and Hammerstein. How could anyone dream up such tunes?

There's much more, of course. Those moments playing in small ensembles when I got "in the zone", when the notes came out as good as I could produce them. Those times when I felt totally in synch with the other musicians, passing musical phrases back and forth. The times I watched Janet perform major roles in operas or sing solo pieces with the Cleveland Orchestra. The times she won

or lost major competitions. The time when I played my own ornamented version of the *Domine Deus* from the Vivaldi Gloria and
managed to end on a difficult high note that had often eluded me
in practice.

I think that all the above experiences were involved in my reactions to the documentary. Yet what made it even more intense was
the contrasting life paths taken by suicide bombers and struggling
musicians, all about the same age, all committed to something bigger than themselves, all part of human history.

May, 2002
Softball in the 40's

I played a lot of baseball from 8 to 12 years old but never used a glove. In Chicago in the forties, we used a large softball, 16 inches in circumference. A standard softball measures 12 inches; for this you need a glove, at least if the ball is new and hard. We used light wooden bats, and whoever showed up got to play.

Games started with two captains choosing up sides. First choice was determined by the captains grasping a bat alternately until one of them reached the knob, and could hold on when the other gave the bat a kick. Younger or handicapped kids were chosen last and were assigned to short center or right field next to someone older. Pitching was underhand and slow, and the batting team usually provided the catcher. The game lasted until dinner time or darkness or heavy rain. Light rain was disregarded.

There were leagues of young men who used the same equipment. We watched them after dinner on summer evenings. Home runs were common for them, but rare for us. A big muscular guy named Bimbo hit at least one homer every game. In our neighborhood he was more popular than Luke Appling, the great White Sox shortstop.

Two more things distinguished that style of baseball from what boys of the same age now play. There were rarely any parents around, and winning wasn't important.

I've watched little league games when my son played, and organized hardball games for younger boys such as my grandsons. They don't look like much fun. There are fathers everywhere. They bring structure and frequent instruction to the younger boys, and a sometimes excessive drive to win to the older ones. The uncoordinated and dreamy and handicapped kids get little more than token playing time.

The changed nature of boys' baseball is partly due to limited playing space in cities and suburbs, partly to an understandable reluctance to let younger boys go more than a block or two away from home without supervision. But a lot has been lost.

The popularity of so-called Windy City softball was that no money was needed to play, so no gloves and no uniforms. It could also be played on small fields with no stands, backstops, umpires, or even bases. In winter we played hockey with sticks and sponge rubber balls on a portion of the same field that the city flooded. Some kids had no skates and used galoshes, the kind with buckles. In the fall, we played touch football.

Boys' sports have changed a lot as structure has taken hold. Sports have been transformed from a game, a social occasion, to a competition. Some think this is a good thing, as it is believed to prepare the boys for the competitive world ahead of them. But competition seems more natural for boys beyond 12 years old, when hormones start working.

The lessons we learned on those delicious summer days were also important for living in the grown-up world. Respect for differences. Fairness. Making decisions without parents around. Dealing with minor injuries. Watching out for younger boys. This is also where we worked out racial and religious integration in our own way. I don't think it would have been as natural or as lasting if our parents were present.

One other difference. Boys now are sorted by age or grade. This is fair if the objective is competition. Yet, there were some advantages to the spread of ages and abilities. Younger kids put up with some teasing in order to learn the game from the older boys. Brothers three or four years apart could play together. Sometimes girls joined us if they wished.

The softball games always had an intermission when the old Greek man with the orange truck drove up. He had cold soda, candy, and hotdogs. If someone had enough money to buy a bottle of orange or grape soda, ten cents I think, a protocol was followed. His teammates could shout "sips", which required a sharing of the soda. Everyone drank from the same bottle, of course. "Bites" was called if a hotdog was purchased. However, it was understood that the purchaser was entitled to at least half of his soda or hotdog. I guess you would call that a social norm. It still makes sense to me.

November, 2002

Fish Stories

In 1950, when I was 15, my friend Alan and I spent many winter afternoons in Chicago looking through fishing tackle catalogs that we had ordered from ads in *Field and Stream*. We did very little actual fishing. In fact, we were purists who believed in removing the barbs from hooks to give fish a sporting chance, and allowing them to go free if you weren't going to eat them. Our main interest was the beauty of the lures in such catalogs as Pflueger and Heddon. We each purchased a small supply of these masterpieces, then filed the barbs off.

In a similar idealistic vein, we insisted on obtaining very light, long casting rods, lines of minimum strength, and high-speed casting reels with balsa wood arbors. We disdained the newly developed spinning rods that allowed fishermen to just keep turning the reel until the fish gave up from exhaustion. If you could actually catch and land a fish with our kind of equipment, you really had won a sporting competition.

It was an unusual pastime for young city dwellers, for there were no fish living anywhere near our neighborhood. In place of fishing, we took to hanging out at the Jackson Park lagoons, where there were organized clubs of men who competed in tournament casting and skish. Tournament casting was simply for distance, while skish involved casting into wooden rings floating at various distances in the lagoon. You used plugs without any hooks for these sports. The men let us try our hands once in a while, but I never won anything.

While accumulating our tackle that winter, we fantasized about a real fishing trip the following summer. We decided the appropriate fish to test our skills and tackle was the fabled smallmouth bass, and we researched the best lakes in the region. We settled on Northern Wisconsin in the Minocqua region, a long day's drive from our homes. For reasons still unknown to me, our parents permitted the two of us to make the trip that summer. Driver's licenses were available at age 15, so the two of us set off in one of our family cars for a three or four day excursion with maps, tackle, and some cash earned through odd jobs.

I think we stayed in a motel, as camping was not our strong point, and we rented a rowboat. We soon found that smallmouth bass were very tough to catch with barbless hooks. In two days of fishing I doubt that we got more than four or five fish into the boat, and the total may have included some small varieties of pan fish. Of course, we threw them all back for another day. It was all rather discouraging, as is so often the case when idealism is tested in the real world.

The trip became memorable when we gave up fishing and wandered into a small carnival one afternoon. Our cash was limited at that point, so we mostly looked around. The most interesting booth was where the operator guessed the age or weight of the customer. If he guessed poorly, the customer was awarded a prize. We hung around most of the afternoon, observing his pitch and guessing ability, both of which were impressive. Late in the day, he chatted with us. He was a graduate student at the University of Wisconsin, making summer income. We must have looked trustworthy, for he asked if we would like to run the booth the next morning while he ran some errands. We could keep any profits we made on good guessing. It didn't take long for us to agree.

He explained the operation. Customers paid either 25 or 50 cents and specified whether they wanted us to guess age or weight. If we failed, they were awarded a kewpie doll worth either 9 or 20 cents. That was the business end. You couldn't lose.

On the operational end, he gave us some important tips. For guessing age, you should first note who came with the customer. Then look at the customer's hands and teeth. Hands and fingernails were the primary key to age, teeth secondary. For weight, the best guide is leg thickness. Finally, there were quite a few Winnebago Indians at the carnival. Apparently they have smaller body cavities than Caucasians, and he told us to add about 20 pounds to our first estimate for them. The last part of our training was learning to lure customers to the booth with a megaphone and a friendly banter, mainly aimed at the women. We practiced these new skills as he consulted.

The next day we took over the booth most of the morning, and we made a few dollars profit as our guessing accuracy gradually improved. We soon learned how to build business volume in slow periods by guessing a few women's age and weight too low, whenever others were standing around, deciding whether to take a chance. I think I did most of the barking, and Alan did most of the guessing. When the proprietor returned, we turned over the money corresponding to the missing kewpie dolls and kept the rest. He was surprised how well we had done, as were we.

We headed back to Chicago having pretty much forgotten smallmouth bass, but full of our first excursion into capitalism.

There's a postscript to this memoir. For many years our family has included wild rice in our traditional Thanksgiving dinner. I've always taken that occasion to explain to my family why wild rice costs so much compared to ordinary white rice. It used to be harvested by Winnebago Indians, gliding through the rice paddies in canoes, beating the plants to gather the grains in the boat. As things happen, an Indian would occasionally fall out of his canoe, head first. Because the Winnebagos are so dense, they can't float on water, so once they are out of the canoe, they're goners. This not only explains why the rice is expensive, but also why you can still see moccasins sticking out of the water in the shallow parts of certain northern lakes, if you look very, very carefully.

February, 2004

The Last Minstrel Show

The *Plain Dealer* recently featured a preview of Cleveland Public Theatre's upcoming production of "Uncle Tom's Cabin", the play based on Harriet Beecher Stowe's best-selling novel of 1852. The play opened in Cleveland in 1853 and was last seen here in the 1930's.

The novel, sometimes described as a poorly written tearjerker, was widely read in America and Europe and had a huge impact on our history. President Lincoln, upon meeting Miss Stowe, was quoted as saying "So this is the little lady who made this big war."

The newspaper's discussion of racial history brought back memories of elementary school and a particular minstrel show. In 1948, I transferred from a public school in Chicago to a private boys' school for 8th grade and high school. I was a good student, and my family believed I would get a better preparation for college there. That point is debatable, but I wasn't ready to stage a rebellion at 13. There is no question that the next five years were different. I was in a class of about 25 boys, all white, several from wealthy families. I had come from a school with boys and girls that was representative of a neighborhood diverse in religion, race, and economic situation.

My public elementary school was one of the very few in Chicago with any real integration, but it was very limited, as the city was still mostly white, over 80%, and blacks were still confined to a few districts. The main arena for integration was sports, in particular the extra-curricular intra-school softball and touch football leagues run by the YMCA. The young adults running and coaching these leagues were graduate students at a local YMCA college that trained future ministers, physical education teachers, and social workers. These twenty-something adults were very progressive-minded, and had a major impact in forming our views about racial integration, fairness, and competition. I remember that our softball team had a black pitcher named Smokey amongst mostly white faces. We were protective of Smokey as we met other, all-white, teams, and not just because he was a terrific athlete – although that probably helped.

Against that background, I found myself among boys whose principal contact with black people was with servants. So, when I learned that our 8th grade stage production that year was to be a minstrel show, I was uneasy. I wasn't sure that I wanted to be part of it. I talked it over with my parents, who encouraged me to take part. They were not totally in accord on the subject of race. My father was more progressive, as he was in manufacturing and relied on a number of black men in running a factory. My mother was more sheltered from the work world and integration. I understood these differences and, even at that age, I knew that times were changing and there would inevitably be generational differences.

I've noticed a similar divergence of parents and children on other social issues, with my own children some years ago and currently as I teach 8th graders at a church Sunday school. Although kids may be woefully ignorant of history, from our perspective of course, they are current on social issues, often well ahead of their parents.

Back to the minstrel show in the spring of 1949. I was cast as the white master of ceremonies known as "Mister Interlocutor", perhaps in recognition of my discomfort, which I had discussed with my teacher. All my co-performers put on blackface and took the traditional roles as jokesters and song-and-dance men. We had a "Mister Bones", a "Mister Tambo", "Zeke", and "Skeeter". I fed them their cues and played straight man.

I obtained some information on minstrel shows from a website of George Mason University. They date to the 1830's, and were performed only by white men in blackface until the Civil War. Some of the famous songs in American history started as minstrel songs: *Dixie, Camptown Races, Oh Susannah,* and *My Old Kentucky Home.* Overall, it seems fair to say they were savage parodies of black Americans but with a fondness for black American culture. They had stock characters such as Jim Crow, Zip Coon, Mr. Tambo, and Mr. Bones. Perhaps out of deference to the changing times, we did not have the first two in our cast – only Mr. Tambo, the happy musician, and Mr. Bones, the percussionist. The first talking picture, "The Jazz Singer" in 1927, was a blackface film. Judy Garland and Bing Crosby did movies with blackface sequences. The minstrel show continued into the mid twentieth century, when it died an appropriate death.

I think enough people in the school besides me found the 1949 production to be outdated, so it was permanently dropped from the 8th grade repertoire. By the 1960's, the boys' school had become an integrated inner city school, and our minstrel show little more than an uncomfortable memory.

January, 2005

The Scandinavian Sofa

On a cold Saturday evening this month, I waited in the car outside a department store while Susan went in for a short errand. I noticed a young couple enter. Suddenly, and surprisingly, a series of memories came over me.

It was 1961 and I was 26. I had a year leave from graduate school in order to manage an engineering field station at an Esso refinery in New Jersey. MIT had three such engineering practice schools for Master degree candidates in Chemical Engineering. My job was to formulate real chemical plant problems for the students, in four separate groups spaced over the school year. I took the job on three weeks' notice.

Relocating from Boston in such a short time with Janet, my wife of three years and a budding opera singer, was feasible as we had no children yet and she had completed her course requirements. A strong incentive was that I would get a real salary as a junior faculty member, $6100 a year if memory serves me. Janet would have a chance to develop professional contacts in New York City.

It was a grand adventure for us both. A new apartment. New friends. Weekend trips to the city in search of museums and cheap restaurants. But the memories that popped up were not these. They were about buying furniture.

We didn't need much for a one-bedroom apartment. We had some used pieces brought from our Boston apartment, a hi-fi system and a lot of records. We had sublet our apartment for the year to another graduate-school couple and left a few things there. Incidentally, the female half of that couple, an aeronautical engineering student, became the Secretary of the Air Force some 30 years later.

This was a typical scene of grad student life, except that for a year we had a little bit of extra money. So we decided to buy a sofa and coffee table, our first real excursion into the world of nest building.

After our initial shock at prices in regular furniture stores, we spent two or three winter evenings at the plentiful discount stores in central New Jersey. Success! We came upon a copy of a Scandinavian sofa with nice blue-striped cushions. The frame was assembled with staples and glue. My guess is we paid about $89, and we added a slightly damaged coffee table, probably no more than $25.

It doesn't seem like much now, and it certainly wasn't much then. But what a thrill it was to buy these things. In the last year, Susan and I have bought some nice furniture for a lot more than $120. We enjoy these too, both because of their quality and because they represent a consensus between us on something for our home. But the pleasure is nothing like that first time.

There are many opportunities for happiness in our lives along with the inevitable sadness. There are the big things: the birth of children, recovery from serious illness and setbacks, acts of unexpected kindness, occasional accomplishments. But certain pleasures are only available at certain times in our lives. At 26, life is open-ended, full of possibilities, fresh and new.

I think it was the feeling of being at the start of something called adult life that sticks with me, not the stapled Scandinavian sofa. When I saw the young couple entering the department store, that feeling came up. Perhaps they were experiencing something similar. I hope so.

May, 2005

Books

Recently I asked the 8th graders in my Sunday school class to prepare a five minute talk on a famous Unitarian or Universalist. The idea was to learn a little history while practicing speaking to the group. Where should they get the material? I mentioned the internet, some easily obtained periodicals, and books. The last suggestion was met with smiles and laughs as if I had told a good joke. Books! Needless to say, the next week we heard a variety of readings from internet downloads, mispronounced words and all. Nobody knew who wrote the pieces they read, or whether they were accurate or controversial.

No doubt they found the fastest way to do the assignment; I might have done the same. Time is as precious a commodity to 13 year olds as it is to their parents. There isn't much of it available amidst schoolwork, team practice, music lessons, walking the dog, television shows, and cell-phone calls to friends. Soon their list will include after-school jobs and the excessively time-consuming game of dealing with the opposite sex. It is often said that the pace of life keeps getting faster and faster, and these kids are no exception.

Reading books for pleasure and instruction is a slow-time pursuit. It has always required giving up something else that takes time, not least including sleep. At a recent social gathering, I chatted with a woman of my generation. We had very little in common, but when the topic turned to reading, we discovered that each of us spent considerable time in our youth reading books with a flashlight under the covers – before television, of course.

Many of us do better gaining knowledge and experience from activity and interaction than from reading and reflection. But a case needs to be made for dreamers, especially those around age 13.

I was a dreamer and a good student, but I didn't have the busy schedule that so many young people have now. In my early teens I got hooked by the novels of Thomas Hardy, and I spent many hours wandering the purple heaths of England in my mind. I explored the Mississippi river with Huck Finn and small-town Indiana with Penrod. All I needed was a library card and an imagination. I can't say that those hours were a great benefit to my future career, but they did feed the dreamer in me. They made me comfortable being alone with myself. I came to like thinking things through, at my own pace.

As a senior in high school I wrote a term paper which was graded in both American History and English. Mine was on the public interactions between Horace Greeley, editor of the New York Herald Tribune, and Abraham Lincoln. I discovered biography and conflicting opinions in many trips to the main Chicago Public Library, a short ride on the "IC" – the Illinois Central commuter line. I filled notebooks and index cards while working at a big table in the main reading room under green-shaded lamps. It was probably the most scholarly piece of non-technical writing I ever did. I learned about bibliographies, footnotes, *ibid* and *op cit*, along with a bit of history.

I came to love libraries. Although I rarely use them anymore, I still experience a special feeling when I wander through stacks of books, frequently pausing to take one off the shelf. It's probably not pure chance that my daughter is a librarian who loves her work.

The special feeling was evident in graduate school when I could spend solitary time in the basement stacks of old journals, digging up obscure articles in various languages. My dissertation was in the field of physical chemistry. I was drawn to papers from the early 20th century in which the authors included hand-drawn graphs and drawings of apparatus embedded in the text. These seemed to create a direct connection between the author and reader that was later weakened when data was presented in professionally drawn graphs printed on separate pages.

That's a special aspect of some books and articles – when you feel the author is talking directly to you. Two important books in my life, which did speak to me, were published around the time I finished my undergraduate education, when I was still quite unsure of my direction in life. One was "The Organization Man" by William Whyte, who was an editor of Fortune Magazine. He wrote about the mid '50's trends toward conformity in business and lifestyle. I recall writing him a note and receiving a gracious reply. The other book was "The Outsider" by Colin Wilson, a series of short biographies of nonconformists such as Albert Camus, William James, and T.E. Lawrence. These two books had much to do with my direction. And yet... doesn't everyone feel like an outsider early in life, and for many, throughout life?

Now I have far too many books in my home, many mostly unread. This creates a persistent, although low-level, sense of guilt. Why did I buy them if I wasn't going to read them? It's too easy to say that most books are not worth reading cover-to-cover, that a quick perusal is enough. There are some partial answers. First, I developed some kind of addiction over the years that prompted me to buy too many books just in case I might find time to read them. Second, it is more difficult to read for long periods as one ages, for the eyes tire all too quickly. Third, my reading interests keep changing. Fourth, I've become more interested in passing on information than in absorbing new material. I think all these are partly true.

So, each year now I vow to get rid of more books than I buy, by donating full cartons to book sales. Maybe, someday, one or two of those 13 year olds will stop at a book sale and get hooked. I wouldn't try to stop them.

October, 2005
30 Years Later

In August, 1975, at age 39, a heart attack sent me home for a couple of months to recuperate. This August, 2005, Susan and I had a quiet dinner out to celebrate the anniversary, as we had done ten years ago in Italy. What, to be specific, was I celebrating? What have I learned?

I started this piece by digging out my 1975 monthly calendar. Yes, I keep them all. Financial records, too. This causes my more spontaneous friends to smile, but I remind them that I still retain a few engineering habits that die hard. Here's what I found.

In the six months leading to the heart attack, I had far too many activities. Two children, 11 and 5, and their priorities. A regular job in industrial research and a side business distributing telephone answering machines. Playing oboe in two orchestras and a baroque ensemble, church board and committee meetings, duplicate bridge and weekend tournaments, extended family church gatherings, and occasional golf. I had a busy professional wife and I was often in charge of the kids, their meals and activities. I think I was even on the board of a community musical organization. There's nothing on this list that I was forced to do.

Although I enjoyed my work and had recorded a few achievements by then, I had little interest in outside engineering-related activities except for an occasional stint as a part-time instructor at a local engineering department. Instead, I spent much energy in music and in people-related church activities. The side business was mostly about the challenge of creating a business. It came close to succeeding, but didn't.

The music had two motivations. First, I had some aptitude for it except for my bad "ear" for pitch. I liked playing well, and had a sense of phrasing and style in early music, in which I had been involved for several years. Second, it was a nice connection with my wife, Janet, a rising professional singer and teacher. We collaborated enough in amateur concerts and home playing to satisfy me. I understood what she was doing and felt part of it.

The people activities had one aspect not available at work, an equality of men and women, which seemed natural to me. I enjoyed participating in discussion groups, whether to solve problems or just air philosophical questions. Most of the time I looked forward to this kind of involvement, and I grew in my ability to work with others.

Within this nonstop schedule, I paid no attention to my health. I thought I could take on anything for which I could find time. I smoked two packs of cigarettes a day. I got by on too little sleep. As a few notes about sick days on my calendar indicate, I paid no attention to early signs of the coming heart attack such as neck and shoulder pain and occasional fatigue. I was astoundingly ignorant about the limitations of the body.

I did not have a mentor. My father had died in 1967 at age 55, and I had no male relatives or older associates who might have cautioned me to find a better, healthier balance in my life. However, I would have needed a very strong influence, for I thought my life was just fine, balanced and productive.

Now I'm 30 years older. Some of those years have been rather turbulent. Job changes, unemployment, two divorces, various ups and downs, but no major health issues. I still love music, but am not actively playing at present. I still enjoy people-related activities, and I had some successes and promotions in my work life along with the jolts in employment. Since retiring 12 years ago, I've become seriously involved in writing plays and essays, and I participate in a few organizations that fit my interests. The pace is much slower than in 1975, but I still get fired up to meet deadlines.

I'm still the same person, but with 30 years of learning tacked on. Or am I? During my recuperation, when I wasn't napping, I often sat near a window and looked at the flowering dogwood outside, trying to make sense of it all. I tell people that having a heart attack at an early age gave me an opportunity to revise my priorities. Certainly, I thought hard about having balance in life, including health issues. I read a lot and thought a lot, but what changes did I really make?

Prior to 1975 I had experienced one unemployment period, so I was reasonably prepared for two more to follow later. Job vulnerability was not a major concern. Divorce and new relationships were not yet in sight. In earlier years, I had shed most of the somewhat compulsive behavior about details that had been amplified back in graduate school. That is, except for keeping calendars and financial records. Thus, any shifts in my thinking after 1975 concerning work, relationships, and personal habits were normal growth processes, not life changing.

Yet, with hindsight, I see that there were two important changes brought about by the heart attack. One was bodily rest. I started getting more sleep and reduced my activities accordingly. Some 15 years later, a physician friend remarked to me that in his judgment there were two root causes of most chronic disease: sleep deprivation and depression. I've come to believe that.

The second change was a gradual shift in attitude. Prior to 1975, I think my primary emotional driver was achievement. It was my default setting, analogous to the routines a computer returns to when restarted. As we move through our days, we temporarily experience the whole range of human emotions: love, disappointment, anger, sorrow, fear, elation, pride, and so on. When the dust settled, my default emotion was something like the satisfaction of achievement.

After the heart attack, I was very grateful to be able to recover from a serious event. As time went on, gratitude worked its way into my outlook on family, relationships, and activities. Naturally,

I pass through all the other emotional states as circumstances change. I still enjoy achievement. But the default setting seems to be a sense of gratitude which, incidentally, is almost the antithesis of depression.

So that's what I celebrate at each anniversary. The lessons that were forced on me by the heart attack. Sleep and gratitude. It seems pretty simple now.

May, 2006
Golf with Jared

Last year I helped my oldest grandson, Jared, get started playing golf. He was 12 years old and had a small assortment of women's-length clubs his parents had picked up. I contributed some lessons with a local teacher, a golf glove, a few golf balls, and a couple of nine-hole rounds.

Before the lessons, we started with a driving range. I tried to simplify the whole process of hitting a golf ball that I have struggled with for too many decades. I said nothing about stance, club choice, or the objective of a golf swing. Just two things. First, I demonstrated how most golfers hold a club – that is, the grip. Second, I advised him to be sure to watch the clubhead hit the ball. Two things to think about are my limit when I swing, so it made golf sense to me.

I congratulated myself when he hit many balls well and surprisingly far. Perhaps I am a natural golf teacher. More likely, he possesses superior eye-hand coordination.

After the lessons, when we played together, I saw something that has improved my own game. When we were near the green, I pointed out that the objective was simply to get the ball as close to the pin as possible. I did not tell him what club to use or how to read greens. Just get it close, which he did most of the time. In fact, it was the best part of his game.

So, I've changed my approach to chip shots for the better. Concentrate on the objective, not on stance, swing, or all the factors that we obsess about. Just get the ball close to the pin. It doesn't matter how.

Keeping the objective in mind is not bad advice for the rest of life, too. I think I'll mention that to Jared.

March, 2007
Justin's Fever

I keep old monthly calendars back into the 1960's, but I can't find this one. It's not likely that I forgot to write it down. It was a Saturday afternoon in the summer of 1969. A lazy, warm Saturday afternoon in Port Washington, Long Island. I was working in a third floor office in our home and Justin, then five years old, was on a cot on a second floor sleeping porch. He had been running a slight fever and I checked him periodically. My wife, Janet, was out on an errand.

Something told me it was time to check Justin. So I did, and found he was in a fever convulsion. His eyes were rolled up, staring at the ceiling and his little body was stiff. All I could think of that moment was potential brain damage. I lifted him up and carried him to the bathroom where I turned on the shower to cold. I stood under the spray, directing it to the back of his neck, both of us completely soaked. I made a short, succinct prayer as his body gradually became limp.

I then carried him outside, shouting for help. A kindly neighbor, an Episcopal priest, ran over, got his car, or maybe it was mine, and drove us to a hospital. This is a good story, as Justin recovered quickly, and we brought him home the same day. His brain was not damaged, and he now has seven children of his own to worry about.

Of course, this is the kind of event that sticks around for a lifetime. So does the prayer. At the time, I had dismissed organized religion for some 20 years. It was another two years before I discovered a like-minded community in liberal religion. Yet the old teachings hang around. My prayer was directed to some sort of God, if he existed at all. The message was simple. Please help get this boy through this crisis. If you do, I will pay you back, somehow.

I have no idea whether I've kept my part of the bargain. But I haven't forgotten it. Maybe that's the important thing.

High School: A Letter to My Grandsons

Dear Guys:

My two grandfathers led full and complicated lives, like every-one else who lives a few years. It's a shame that I know too little about them. They had some noteworthy accomplishments and some tragic episodes. Because we live in different times, their lives were as different from mine as my life will be different from yours. Yet, many things stay the same over the generations. How we deal with the people around us. What principles we use in making deci-sions. How we deal with the very good and the very bad events that come our way.

I've written around 100 personal essays in recent years, and I intend to keep at it. If you find time to read them someday, you will get a better sense of the course of my life than I have about my grandparents. Some of the essays will be more interesting than others, but you'll be the judges.

This letter is about an outstanding opportunity available to you that was also available to me, but not to my grandfathers. It's called high school.

Around 1900, not many boys finished high school. Boys went to work early to support themselves and often their families, whether on farms or in cities. Most further education was self-education or on-the-job training. Public libraries were vital in this process.

In my parents' generation, completion of high school became much more common, though far from universal. Public education was a well supported community value in our country, perhaps the most important foundation for our prosperity in the 20th century. Both my parents went on to college. My mother finished a Bachelor's degree in English, while my father dropped out to start work during the dark days of the depression. I continued the family trend by going on to graduate school for professional education, as did many other people. This is not to say that more and more formal education is better – only that it is an important option to be considered for certain careers. There are other ways to become an educated person capable of making intelligent decisions in life. That is the goal.

High school. First, let's list the special problems you will face before the opportunities. You will grow one or two inches a year, your voices will drop as you mature physically, you will spend far too much time thinking about girls and what they think of you, and you will be tempted by dangerous or illegal pursuits. You will encounter kids who are much better than you in some skill you are trying to develop. There is <u>always</u> someone better, by the way, whether in athletic skill, intellectual prowess, musical or artistic talent, or ability to attract girls. You may find yourself in a group that does things you find questionable, and you will have to decide whether to join them or not. None of these problems disappear at the end of high school, so it's good training for later years.

If the problems were all that high school offered, it would be a dismal prospect indeed. Here's the other part of the story. You will have three or four years to grow in so many ways that it's like making choices in a candy store. Here are a few examples and a few memories of my time in high school. Keep in mind that I attended a small all-boys high school, so I didn't have the daily distraction of girls in the classroom. It was also a bit more competitive academically than a large co-ed school. Both of these things were probably good for me, but not for everyone. I don't think I would have turned out much differently had I gone to a large school, but I can't say for sure.

Choosing subjects: I didn't have much choice since we were all on a college-bound track. Don't take easy stuff because it is easy. It's also a waste of your time. You need to find out what you are good at, and stretch yourself. When I was at MIT, I had a physics professor who believed that advanced theoretical science courses were for students in their twenties, not teens. He thought that the best courses for teens were those full of information to be absorbed, for instance languages, botany, and literature. (He was from Switzerland and told us how he learned the names of <u>all</u> the wildflowers in the mountains near his home as a teenager.) I don't totally agree with that, but it's good food for thought.

Science and Math: Keep the door open to a possible career in science or engineering by taking the best courses available. I enjoyed my career as a chemical engineer in industrial research and development, and your father enjoys being a computer engineer, also in industry. If you find you have the aptitude for it, and you <u>like</u> solving technical problems, it is certainly worth considering. Catch me another time, and I'll be glad to give you my opinions about the many paths you might take in a science-based career.

Foreign Language: High school is a great time to learn to speak a foreign language or two. It does require putting in study time every day, a very good habit to acquire. You will be part of a much more international world than I have been, so it makes good sense now. I took four years of Latin, not a spoken language. However, I greatly enjoyed gaining some understanding of ancient history and reading famous works in the original language. Most important, I had to put in an hour every night preparing my lesson. (One year I was the only one in the class, so no excuses!) When I got to college, I found that I had a better habit of studying than most the students around me. It was from Latin.

Literature: Read lots of novels and short stories and poetry. Lots. Unless you go on to major in literature, you will have more reading time in high school than any equivalent period the rest of your life. One suggestion: memorize some favorite poems. Another: read something to increase your vocabulary. When I was 14 or 15 I found, by accident, a paperback book entitled "30 Days to a More Powerful Vocabulary." When I got through that, I felt much more like an adult.

Speaking: Find occasions when you have to stand up in front of people, most often your classmates, and give a speech. It's a special skill that needs to be practiced, and it is useful whatever you do.

Sometimes there is a minor class available in high schools in public speaking, or a debating society. Look into it.

Writing: Take every opportunity to write, and seek good criticism of your writing, not just from teachers. That includes all forms: essays, reports, fiction and scripts, research papers. To be able to express yourself in words is extremely valuable whatever you end up doing. During my senior year in high school, I had to do an original research paper covering both my English and American History classes. I chose to write about Abraham Lincoln and the editor of the New York Tribune, Horace Greeley. I spent many hours at the Chicago Public Library reading books and articles, and I learned how to handle references, bibliographies, and all the stuff that makes a research paper. It was tedious and time consuming, but the result was worth it. Note: We have one of the best public libraries in the country in downtown Cleveland, an easy ride on the Rapid.

Music, Art, and Athletics: My school was too small to offer music and art courses, and I didn't learn to play an instrument. I had to catch up later in life. However it is available, develop your skills in these areas. Even if they are not what you decide to specialize in later in life, a grounding in music and art makes for a better life. So does working on your athletic skills. You already know that sports are not only fun, they help you get your body in shape and learn the importance of teamwork – which is valuable in much of life outside sports.

I'm always available to talk more about this or other subjects. Keep me posted on your high school experience – both problems and opportunities. I probably have some more stories, too.

Love, Grandpa Bill

October, 2008

Tap Dancing

I suppose my fantasies exist for a few brief moments much like yours. They surface most often just before falling asleep, less often while daydreaming. The particulars are my own, but surely they resemble the dream sequences of others who have their own fantasy buttons. Perhaps the most common, for a guy, involves an attractive female, real or imagined, whose interest is piqued by some accomplishment or nugget of wisdom on his part. To set that one off requires little more than reasonable health and a few hormones.

Other fantasies respond to other ordinary personal needs. If hungry, it isn't remarkable to imagine a feast of favorite foods. If facing an important or stressful event, an imagined successful outcome provides a few pleasant moments of fantasy before the return to reality. Less obvious parts of our personality, and the fantasies they support, are more interesting because they differentiate us. They make you you and me me.

One of my special fantasies is dancing like Fred Astaire with one of his glamorous partners, on a glistening stage or ballroom floor, in view of rapt onlookers. This fantasy collided with reality last summer when I took a one-week course in tap dancing with fifteen others at Omega Institute in Rhinebeck, New York. First, some personal history.

My life in dance started with a class in ballroom dancing for 30 or 40 seventh graders, about which I had very little choice. I was quite apprehensive about girls, but I found the dancing part was not difficult. The class was run by Mr. Mayhew at a hotel ballroom in Chicago. He started and stopped each dance and lesson with a pair of castanets. To make sure that the boys were prompt to ask girls to dance when the castanets clicked, Mr. Mayhew promised to be the partner, himself, for any boy who did not find a girl. The system worked.

In my early teens I was enrolled in a group that sponsored monthly dances, and I found I liked the dancing more as I slowly shed my concerns about girls. In fact, I became fairly proficient at it, and did my share of showing off on the dance floor in subsequent years. At the same time I discovered jazz, and a few years later, classical music. To this day I still love the rhythms of cool jazz along with classical. I find my foot tapping to a Mozart allegro as well as to Dave Brubeck.

When I was about 14, a neighbor offered his drum set for sale before heading off to college. This was an exciting prospect, but my father vetoed it. He had listened to drum practice through open basement windows for too long to allow it in his own house. At the time I accepted that, but in retrospect it was unfortunate, as I later realized that drumming would have been a perfect fit for my musical aptitude, which was just beginning to form.

Around the same time, the early 1950's, I saw some of the great dance movies of Hollywood, mostly from MGM. Some more than once. Fred Astaire was still active, and Gene Kelly was riding high. *American in Paris* and *Singing in the Rain* were from this era. I don't think those two have ever been surpassed.

In my twenties and thirties, I learned to play recorder and taught some community classes in playing renaissance music. Recorder playing and recorder music are technically fairly simple compared with modern instrumental music. However, the aspect of that music that draws many players is the interesting, and sometimes complex, rhythmic forms.

About ten years ago, in my early 60's, I bought a pair of tap shoes and took a local community program in tap for beginners. Not enough people showed up to keep it going, but I got a taste for it. So, last summer I signed up for the course at Omega Institute.

One memorable feature of the class was the excellent young instructor, a 23 year old man, and his passion for the history of tap. Each day we spent an hour or so looking at film clips of the great tap dancers, starting with Bojangles and Shirley Temple. I enjoyed the week, but age has taken its toll on my balance and agility, and my shoes were a half size too short. After an hour or two spent learning steps each day, my toes wanted to quit. We managed to put on a choreographed performance for the other campers at the end of the week. I struggled, but I count it a milestone in my life.

Why do tap dancing, and more generally, dance rhythms, appeal to me? I can't identify a genetic heritage for this trait, but it must be there. I might as well ask why I am fearful of heights, take easily to mathematics, or have a weak visual memory.

Consistent with my mathematical orientation, I have come to think of most ordinary personality characteristics as normally distributed in the population, on a 1-10 scale, say. For most traits, we score in the midrange, 4 to 7. For example, I'd judge myself an 8 on rhythmic sense and a 2 on dealing with heights. Whichever side of the curve we fall on, it is certainly possible to move up with education, training, and practice. But not far. It seems a much better use of time and effort to fine-tune the traits where we start with a high score. That is, build on our strengths. Folk wisdom supports this in many ways, as not making silk purses out of a sow's ear.

It is important that we explain differences in personal characteristics to children in some such way, perhaps without the math. As kids, we tended to think poorly of those who couldn't run as fast or spell as accurately. To understand that these differences are innate is an important step in growing up.

So, in our brief departures from reality, you can imagine slam-dunking like LeBron James while I tap my way across a stage like Fred Astaire.

May, 2009
Falling For Life

I've had two minor falls in the last year. I was trotting to a putting green during a golf game and caught my foot on a low rope, pitching forward; instantly, I went into a forward roll or somersault and rose with no problem. The other time I sat on a bench situated on a low slope; it gave way and I rolled over backwards, also with no serious problem. In both cases, the people nearby were quite surprised. There have been several other falls in the last 50 years with no injury beyond some minor scrapes and bruises. I owe these favorable outcomes to a few months of judo training 60 years ago, when I was 13, in the eighth grade.

In the fall of 1948, Arthur, a fellow eighth grader, told me he was planning to take judo lessons and asked if I wanted to join him. After discussing it with my father, I signed up. Once a week for a few months we took a bus after school through the South Side in Chicago to a run-down building just south of the Loop, where John, a high level black belt, taught in a basement studio. John was Japanese-American, in his thirties, and had recently won prizes at the Pan-American games.

Half of each lesson consisted of learning falls, and half learning throws and chokes, which Arthur and I practiced on each other. Sometimes we had to practice with John, who was difficult to throw and impossible to choke. Neither of us enjoyed the physical contact and falling at first, but after a few weeks it became more comfortable. We also were gaining some self confidence, which we did enjoy. The next spring, John encouraged us to enter a city-wide competition with other beginners. That wasn't much fun, and I subsequently retired from competition.

I matured late. Two years later, when I got my first driver's license at age 15, I was still 135 lbs and 5 ft 6 in. When I graduated from high school at 17, I was 6 ft 1 in., a growth of 7 inches in two years. At 13, I envied the boys who were beginning to show signs of growth and I wondered more than once if I would ever grow up. I was also unhappy with roughhousing and games of touch football where we did everything except tackle the runner without any padding. The judo training gave me a considerable boost in my physical self confidence to the point that I didn't look for excuses to avoid physical contact. That was a real gain.

My career in judo ended during that eighth grade year, so I am very surprised that the falling lessons have lasted my whole life, somewhere deep within my muscle memory. John knew what he was doing.

June, 2009

My Life in Jazz

In the summer of 1981 I drove south to a college campus in Louisville for a week at a jazz camp run by Jamey Aebersold. I had my 1938 alto sax, some fresh reeds and a pleasant anticipation about the week. Aebersold published music-minus-one LP records for aspiring jazz musicians, and I had seen ads for his workshops. Although I could play written music reasonably well on the sax, it was time for me to learn something about playing and improvising jazz. I had never studied it formally, as my music experience to that point had been studying and playing recorders in early music, and oboe in baroque and classical music. But I had always loved jazz and had some feel for it.

The situation was not quite what I expected; I thought there would be more beginners. There were over 80 students, nearly all male, with a median age of about 19. At 45, I was 3rd or 4th oldest, and I was 3rd or 4th least experienced, topped only by some players trying a new instrument. The faculty was a group of professional musicians from New York City, most of them proficient at more than one instrument. The largest number of students were wind players with a scattering of pianists, drummers, and a couple of bass players. Even the teenagers had a fair amount of playing experience including some paid gigs. Some of them were very good; two were outstanding. I found it hard to keep up with even casual conversations, for there is a special language among jazz musicians that I did not know, just as in any group of professionals. It was OK that I was a beginner, but that did not give me much comfort.

During the week we lunched at tables along with faculty members. I recall one time when I sat next to a trumpet player from New York. I asked him how many hours a day he played trumpet, and he said about 6 or 7 hours unless he had to eat or install an air conditioner. I remarked that 7 hours seemed like a lot to me. He said that he then played a gig every evening. I think of that conversation when I hear professionals play what sounds effortless.

On the day of arrival, we auditioned for a teacher in order to be placed in an appropriate small group or combo for the week. After I played a few scales for the teacher, he asked me to name my favorite sax player. That was easy – Paul Desmond, Dave Brubeck's collaborator who had died just four years before. The teacher paused, looked at me quizzically, wrote down a note, and ended the audition. I later understood that Desmond and his cool jazz style were out of favor among New York jazz musicians, who were immersed in the bebop style and its successors. So that was not a great start to the week. In retrospect, Desmond's unique sound, "like a dry martini" as he said, is timeless while bebop derivatives have come and mostly gone.

I was placed in one of two beginner groups, distinguished from all the others by not having its own rhythm section (piano, drums, and bass). We had two saxes, two flutes, and one trumpet. We had a good teacher, a tenor sax player, and worked on basics: scales, reading chord changes, ear training, etc. Each afternoon we practiced alone or rehearsed to play on the last evening of the workshop in front of our fellow students. The faculty concert was on the next-to-last evening.

Here is where being in the beginners group paid off. We got to play with a complete faculty rhythm section instead of students. Our teacher carefully chose a piece for us that had no chord changes: "Sugar" by Stanley Turrentine, entirely in one blues-scale key. That meant we could stand up to do a solo using only one scale. I practiced that scale over and over. When the time came to play my solo of two or three choruses, I managed an acceptable rendition and variations. My new friends, who knew of my struggles that week, cheered wildly. It was all worth it.

SCIENCE, CONSCIOUSNESS, and SPIRITUALITY

June, 1998
My Affair with S

I've had a few years of singleness in my adult life, so I admit to a modest number of personal relationships, some of longer duration and others shorter. A few, within my limited experience, were tumultuous. For the record, my current marriage is remarkably solid, frequently joyous, the result of great good fortune.

Yet I've had another very long-term affair, much longer than any of the others, from which I have drawn considerable support and nourishment. She has always been hovering in the background, ready to take care of me whenever my circumstances became clouded with emotional entanglements or indecision. She has provided me confidence and support for much of my useful work in the world.

Her name is Science, S for short. S and I have been attached intimately for many decades, and I am willing to admit that I have taken her for granted too often. So, it's only right that I express my gratitude here in public for this lifetime relationship, and I hope that in my small way I have paid her back.

Why this avowal now? Because the affair has cooled in recent years. To put it bluntly, I've lost some confidence in S. I should say *S as I have known her,* for the problem may be my perception of S, not her real nature. However, I can say that my perception of S is that which is held by most scientists. A fine dilemma, indeed. Does S have an essential nature *different than* the way she is generally perceived by scientists? Let's return to that one later. Notwithstanding my remarks in this brief confession, I still yearn for her return and I hope we can work out our differences.

What has come between us? The simple answer is certain real-life experiences that seem to be of no interest to S. Things that cause eyebrows to be raised among S's friends; things that elicit remarks such as "What in the world have you been reading lately?" or "Baloney" or "Show me the double blind studies." Or worse.

A non-scientist might ask a pertinent question at this point. Aren't all things in this world covered by the umbrella of science, somehow or other? It's a good question, one that might be asked by a musician or a historian. The answer seems to be no.

Science is a continual striving for verifiable truth. It is based, ultimately, on observation and controlled experiment. Of course, both observations and experiments can be less than perfect, and scientific truths periodically undergo shifts as better observations and experiments are performed. I'm not even including the many instances where science is twisted to make a point, or deliberately falsified to make a buck.

I vividly remember my few encounters with Doc Lewis early in my career and very late in his. Lewis was a founder of chemical engineering, my 30 year profession, in the early 1900's. I once saw Doc in action when he had a graduate student stand up in class. "Mr. Jones, do you believe in Boyle's Law?" That is the simple notion that, for a confined gas, the pressure goes up when volume goes down and vice versa, in exact proportion. Mr. Jones, with some caution, answered yes. Doc then moved in for the kill: "Why?" Poor Jones, as the rest of us would, started to expound on the kinetic theory of molecules, or perhaps the mathematics of the perfect gas law, and Doc stopped him quickly. Those were theories, he pointed out. Boyle's Law, like all of science, was based on experimental observations. Theories came later. Science is grounded in observation.

For many years I operated my professional life and much of my personal life on this simple basis: good science is the path to truth and it is grounded in observable facts. That is, things that humans (or their instruments) can see, hear, touch, smell, or taste.

I haven't been disappointed in the results. I certainly had my share of professional accomplishments that relied on working out the consequences of solid scientific laws.

I should note that I had an excellent education, and a natural inclination for applied science – how things work and how to design things that work, and how to describe all this mathematically. Most of the groundwork for my particular range of knowledge was developed before the 20th century. I am largely ignorant of major advances of this century in such things as quantum physics, solid state chemistry, molecular biology, astronomy, and countless other disciplines. Still, I have been exposed to many awesome accomplishments of the scientific method in such disparate things as why rivers form snakelike paths, how fuels burn, why certain chemical reactions happen and others don't, and how to describe a series of random events.

The challenges to my affair with S have come mainly in three areas: intuition, healing, and psychic phenomena.

Some time ago I found I was a pretty good predictor or estimator. Although trained in applied science, I guess I'm more an engineer at heart, in that I always liked making decisions with incomplete information – more an art form than scientific reasoning. Engineers tend to work under the pressure of insufficient data and time, and that fit me. It occurred to me late in this game that I was relying on some kind of intuitive input, the old "gut feel". Certainly this is partly explained by having a large storehouse of subliminal information to draw on, but not entirely. Now I think that I was often tapping into something beyond my stored knowledge. I can't say much more about it, except that it became almost a routine way to function as the years went on. In personality tests I've scored strongly intuitive – like millions of other people – and this seemed consistent with my experience.

I've also participated in workshops on using the "right side of the brain" for writing poetry – one-person brainstorming, perhaps. I was surprised at the production of ideas that resulted.

I know little about dream interpretation, but that is a well-regarded route to intuitive knowledge.

July, 1990. I sit in a discussion group at a summer workshop and hear a young woman tell an amazing story. She is married, has three young children and an MBA, and has a very busy life as a bank consultant. That year she discovered she was a healer. She would get an image of a ball of energy over her head into which she could dip her hands. In that state she found she could bring about significant healing of chronic medical conditions in relatives and close friends, although she was apprehensive about working with strangers. S told me to be skeptical, but my strong sense was that this woman was reporting a truthful experience, probably accurately.

Subsequently, I read that her image is one of three described by energy healers. Hardly any healers have a coherent explanation for their peculiar ability; it just comes to them, like hitting home runs comes to a few lucky young men.

The power of prayer in healing has been studied and documented in recent years. Although many scientists are willing to acknowledge that it is often effective, the usual reasoning is that it has to do with the psychological effect on the patient which, in turn, causes internal physical changes. Undoubtedly that is part of the truth, as our biochemical selves are rapidly being revealed in all their complexity. So that seems to be the Scientific truth. Yet is it the whole truth? People who pray are not doing it to manipulate the patient's psychology, but to connect the patient with universal forces. Just because we can't measure them, do they not exist?

September, 1997. I am attending a week-long workshop with 200 others, listening to Caroline Myss talk about intuition. Myss is a medical intuitive, a rare person who can "read" a person's state of health over a long distance phone, given only the person's name and age. At the conference I saw her do that dozens of times with incredible accuracy, sitting at least 60 feet away from the subject. With no prompting, she told people about their physical and emotional conditions, their past operations and states of healing, their concerns about children and parents, the state of their marriages or relationships. She claims to perceive energy transmissions from different parts of the body (the chakra system) in a way that has been totally natural to her for a long time.

At the workshop as well as in her books and tapes, Myss has described many other unusual phenomena such as out-of-body experiences, and reports of bilocation and conversations with deceased persons by others.

Although I had read casually about psychic phenomena, I had never seen it happen in front of me. It was remarkable. It cannot be explained by any science I was aware of. But it was real; of that I'm sure.

I did not volunteer to be read by Caroline Myss but I felt some kind of connection to her nonetheless, with only a few remarks exchanged between us. To this day I wonder if she read me.

After returning home, I began to speak with friends about what I had seen and experienced. To my surprise, I found that many people have had psychic experiences, but they are reluctant to talk about them. They are not acceptable topics in the casually scientific culture in which we live.

Back to a question posed earlier, stated slightly differently. Must Scientific Truth be limited by its reliance on sensory observation – that is, the five human senses? Or is the *practice* of Science the problem? Surely the experiences I have sketched have a valid reality in the same world that Science attempts to explore. Why not include intuition and psychic phenomena and prayer, and a host of other nonsensory observations, in the list that must be incorporated in any inclusive explanation of the world?

Much like memories of an earlier lover, I'll never really get over my long affair with S. But we have grown apart. What's that? I didn't fully appreciate her? *She* always had the capacity to accept intuition and all the other inputs. It was *I* who bought into the world as constructed by Scientists? And rather than upset me, she let me find my own way. So... why don't I just drop over some evening and we can talk it over?

Let me think about it.

September, 2000

Images

We live by images. Are they the real thing? Those of us with sight find it easy to believe that the images that form in our brain from light waves that enter our eyes represent reality. Seeing is believing. What you see is what you get. It's plain as day.

With slightly more sophistication, we admit that a magician with quick hands can fool our eyes; that darkness can lead us to imagine that we see things that aren't there; that different witnesses often see a crime scene differently, at least in their memories.

Most of us have also thought a little about what we might see if our eyes responded to infrared wave lengths or X-rays instead of visible light, and we have seen images that result from those transmissions. Those of us who grew up in the mid twentieth century remember seeing the bones of our feet with an X-ray device at the local shoe store.

Still, these are exceptions. Most of the time we are quite certain that the things we see in plain sight are the only reality we need to be concerned about.

There's another way *to look at this*, and the play on words is intentional. We know that our brain forms the image we see, largely but not entirely from sensory input from the eyes. Input from touch is fairly easy to understand. Reach into a drawer or a crowded refrigerator or a purse. Your fingers help create an image of the object, sometimes by joining with a visual memory rather than a view in present time. The other senses work similarly. Blind people form images, too, sometimes entirely from touch and memory.

Another very important source of input to our images beyond our five senses and our stored memories is intuitive or psychic input. This is much easier to experience than to explain. For present purposes, I'll make three assertions that I believe to be true, but I won't try to convince you.

1. We all have an active intuitive sense. We differ on how active or how accurate.

2. Intuitive knowledge does not come from stored data in our brains, but from a nonphysical realm that is present everywhere.

3. We are rarely aware of the blend of intuitive and sensory inputs that shape our images.

One of my favorite demonstrations of the brain's use of non-sensory input is hypnosis. In a case related by the author Michael Talbot, a man volunteered to be hypnotized in a home setting among friends, by an expert in the field. He was told that when he awoke, he would not be able to see his teenage daughter, who was in the same room. Upon waking, he could not see her a few feet away. The hypnotist then went behind her and held his pocket watch behind her back. The father could read the time and inscription right through his daughter's body. In this special case of hypnosis, the light wave data picked up by the subject's eyes was overridden by a hypnotic suggestion, not by physical or intuitive input.

Intuitive input plays a role in many ordinary activities, but it is rarely given credit in things like business decisions, purchases, or driving a car. It's more evident when we change our behavior as a result of a hunch or a gut feeling, particularly in dealing with people. Even then, we prefer to call it experience rather than intuition.

I've written elsewhere about my experience with "remote viewing", a psychic activity that takes some practice to achieve a reasonable level of competence. A target, usually a photo of some place in the world for learning purposes, is given a number. Viewers attempt to gain information about the target knowing only the number assigned to it. The method involves quieting the conscious mind through meditation or other means in a quiet place, then focusing on the number and recording the images that arise.

In order to explain remote viewing, and a number of other demonstrated psychic phenomena, one has to start with a statement such as No. 2 above, namely the existence of some kind of nonphysical information realm from which image material is drawn.

Let's turn to two very ordinary, daily exercises in image making – reading and dreaming.

People who read a lot as children, especially novels, often remark that they do not get the same level of pleasure from movies or television as from books. This common remark may have to do with images. When reading books, we make our own images – and they do not come only from the printed words, but also from memory and (I believe) from intuitive input. Movies and television images leave much less to our imaginative processes, and seem weaker. More lifeless perhaps.

In dreams, we are totally cut off from material passing through our eyes, and the images are often bizarre and wildly imaginative. If you believe in intuitive input at all, you must conclude that dreams are rich in it. Does this input come from outside the brain? Can it arise from someone else's experience, not just our own? In his standup comic days, Woody Allen told how he was knocked unconscious in a bicycle accident. He lay on the street, his whole life passing before his eyes: the log cabin, the gingham curtains, and the sheep grazing nearby. Only when he awoke did he realize it was someone else's life.

Yes, images are real. They certainly exist. But they are made of many pieces of information besides what passes through our eyes. There is growing evidence that much of this information comes from somewhere other than our brain cells.

May, 2001

The Radio Analogy

In many ways, we are like radio receivers as we function in the familiar world around us. Maybe it is more accurate to say that radios are like us, as we came first. After all, our technologies are, for the most part, extensions of skills already known to us. The radio analogy may be helpful as we explore the unfamiliar nonphysical world, also all about us.

Radio transmissions surround us, envelop us, and pass through us continually. Yet, in order to hear our favorite station, we not only need a receiver, but must attach it to a source of electrical power, warm it up, and tune it to the right frequency. Moreover, we need to be in a location where our station's frequency is not overwhelmed by natural disturbances or by another station on the same or nearby frequency.

Radio reception is very familiar, yet its workings are still mysterious to most of us. We probably know that the theory of radio was worked out over a century ago in one of the most creative milestones of physical science. Many of its terms have entered common speech. We say, for instance, that two people who converse well are "on the same wave length". We admire a professional athlete who can "tune out" many distractions and focus on hitting a baseball or making a basket.

In fact, our survival and ability to function in the physical world depend on our capacity to tune in to the right frequency in routine activities such as driving a car, in listening to verbal instructions, or in paying attention to danger. We do these things despite hundreds of possible distractions, from physical discomfort to memories of this morning's argument.

Warming up is another very familiar activity – in sports or in playing a musical instrument, for example. A good teacher helps a class warm up before presenting difficult material. A common problem for secondary or college students is when there is no time to warm up after a hurried dash from literature to math class.

Good presenters know how to prepare an audience. Religious services often start with a meditation to bring the congregation into the moment and out of their worldly concerns. An effective way to start a discussion group is with a "check-in", where participants warm up by opening up to the group.

One other radio analogy, filtering, closely relates to tuning. We filter out significant but extraneous signals that would otherwise obscure what we wish to receive, or must receive for our survival. People who do well in crises are able to filter in a chaotic environment so that they may fine tune their response in the most useful way. Emergency medical workers and combat soldiers often show this ability, the result of good training.

However, training is sometimes less than perfect and can lead us down an erroneous path. It is based on the way things have been in the past, and that may not be the way they are now or in the future. Two of the most important sources of training for most of us are education and organized religion. Close behind are our personal histories, our experience.

I believe that our worldly training is deficient in preparing us to deal with the nonphysical world, the realm of the spirit – at least in the modern Western world. This world took shape in the 17th century, perhaps best defined by the philosopher Descartes. He proposed a dualism, wherein the world's knowledge is divided into separate realms overseen by science (the physical world) and religion (the nonphysical). The net effect was the emergence of physical science as the principal Western philosophy, and the long, slow decline of the influence of organized religion on modern thinking.

Science has two faces, however. One is the large body of theory and experiment that has done an astonishing job of describing the physical world, generating countless technologies and insights into *things* from subatomic particles to the known cosmos. The other face is an attitude of exploration that keeps observing the world, looking for a more consistent description and deeper understanding, always respectful of data – particularly those that do not easily fit existing theories. The first face is the one that forms the prevalent Western belief system, our *de facto* religion. Its big drawback is that it has no place for the nonphysical world.

A few scientifically minded people are probing the nonphysical part of the universe. Whatever their credentials in the physical scientific world, many first class, they exhibit the second face of science. I find their efforts not only fascinating, but very exciting in the opening up of new understandings of ourselves and our place in the universe.

Returning to the radio analogy, here are a few thoughts about this exploration. First, three assertions that I will not attempt to prove or support in this brief essay.

1. There is a universal nonphysical part of the world that is not subject to the current laws of physics.

2. It intersects the physical world in countless ways, in such common experiences as intuition, dreaming, healing, and creative activity.

3. It has been demonstrated in scientifically sound experiments as well as a huge number of recorded individual experiences.

I also think it is logical, but perhaps that betrays my scientific bias.

It is difficult to access the nonphysical world consciously and purposefully, but easy to do in an undirected, often random way – as in dreaming. Even if you find a way into it, through deep meditation or other practice, it remains very hard to extract insights and collect them in the conscious mind so that they may be expressed in language. Most often, the best result we can obtain is a gut feeling or emotional shift.

Our difficulty seems to have a lot to do with the *filters* constructed from our education and worldly experiences. Children find it easier. Nonscientific primitive tribal people find it easier. Our prescientific ancestors found it easier.

So, the first step in accessing the nonphysical world is to have an appropriate radio receiver and *turn it on*. For most people this is the hardest step. It means remodeling your belief system to allow for the possibility of something more than FM, AM, and short wave bands, and then making the effort to try it out. Why bother? My only answer is, why restrict yourself to the physical world, in the face of counsel and advice from the greatest thinkers of history in all wisdom traditions?

The next step is *warm-up*. Besides the obvious preliminary step of minimizing distractions, spiritual practices accomplish this for many accessors. Meditating, singing, chanting, dancing, praying, fasting, and many other disciplines qualify. Underlying all of these is the intentional practice of getting present – getting your mind out of the past and the future and existing in the "now".

Finally, *tuning in*. This may simply mean opening up to the nonphysical world and letting yourself experience it. It may also mean very directed concentration on some topic of interest, where you are seeking guidance. It may also mean connecting with another person, as in some healing practices.

It has been found that we have some built-in filters that screen out certain kinds of information, even if we are able to achieve meaningful and purposeful access to the nonphysical world. Psychologists understand these as blocks. There is a recorded account of an experienced and productive remote viewer who was able to pick up psychic information about distant targets on demand, a high percentage of the time. However, he never was able to see weapons in any scene, which he could describe with remarkable accuracy otherwise. He always filtered out weapons subconsciously, and understood that he did.

Probing the nonphysical world through our minds, and building an understanding of the process, is a great frontier for discovery, both personal and scientific.

But first, you need to get the right kind of radio.

January, 2002
My Short Life as a Medium

In the fall of 2001, I took a course in mediumship over three weekends at Lilydale Assembly in western New York State near Lake Chautauqua. Lilydale is a Spiritualist camp of the same 19th century vintage as the Chautauqua Institution. It fronts on a quiet lake, and has modest summer cottages on a few streets, assembly halls, and two Spiritualist churches. Most of the homes are owned by psychic mediums who are available all summer for readings. A few live there year around. In the summer season, there are many workshops and courses, and public events every day, including free, short readings indoors and outdoors. It is a pleasant and peaceful place to spend a day, whatever your views on Spiritualism.

Susan and I had visited Lilydale in the two preceding years, motivated by our continuing interest in consciousness and spirituality. We had also attended an appearance by the nationally known psychic, Sylvia Browne, in Cleveland. In the spring of 2001 we heard a talk by Professor Gary Schwartz of the University of Arizona about a research study of mediums. He had assembled five mediums with good reputations from all over the U.S., and had them do readings on the same persons, with no interaction among them. His published results show remarkable consistency among the five. It would take an extremely resistant skeptic to discount them, but many do.

After our first visit to Lilydale, we talked with a friend, a minister. She had taken a summer course there and was very positive about the results. Since then, when she does a memorial service, she routinely asks the deceased what he or she wants said during the service.

Psychics have an above-average ability to perceive information from a nonphysical source, as we all do in dreams or intuitive moments. Mediums are a small subset of psychics who communicate with the dead, most often relatives of the person having the reading. Susan and I have had some psychic experiences in remote viewing and medical intuition, with assistance from experienced teachers in workshop situations. I was ready to learn how mediums work.

My class had ten women and one other man. We covered a lot of material about symbolism, since psychic information most often appears in symbolic terms. We were told to develop our own psychic dictionaries of colors, numbers, and images – even sound and odor sensations. If I sense dark red, for instance, I might find, after some experience, that it means anger to me, while to someone else it might mean blood. We also learned various ways to meditate and concentrate, and did many exercises, alone and with each other. We practiced reading each other. One of the useful instructions for doing readings was to have a simple mental checklist of topics that people are interested in, and work through it. For example, health, career, finance, or relationships. Through all of this, our teacher frequently repeated the need to strive for our highest level of intention and honesty.

The core of the process is to find ways such as meditation to clear the conscious mind out of the way, so you can receive information. In other words, allow information to come to you. This teaching is nearly identical to guidelines we had received in remote viewing. Get the conscious mind out of the way by a disciplined approach; then let it happen.

We had homework to do between weekends. At one time I asked Susan to put five photographs of people I know in sealed envelopes. I then went through meditation and mind-clearing exercises before gathering impressions about the contents of the envelopes. For three of them, my impressions made no sense to me. The fourth was a grandson in an antique house setting. I picked up oldness and old woodwork, which were accurate. The fifth was my sister in front of our old family home in Chicago during a trip two years ago. I had a fairly clear image of a young man playing a banjo, and I assumed it was a banjo-playing contemporary of mine. When I opened the envelope, I saw that it could have been our father who died 35 years ago. As a young man he played banjo, something my sister did not even know, but the kind of image that would give me a specific reference. Although I was disappointed overall, I guess 40% is not bad.

Our personalities and experience naturally play important roles in our results. Late in the course we were led through a long meditation. At the end we were asked to envision our personal guide or gatekeeper to the psychic universe, and to sketch this figure. Everyone but me had mythical figures, all male. Some looked liked Old Testament prophets, some were animals, and some were part human, part animal. I was a little reticent to show mine, a modern guy with a funny hat and a T-shirt labeled "gatekeeper". Around him were charts of symbols, bottles of cures, and a shelf of record books. His name was Leonard. I've never been big on mythology.

On two Sundays I attended a Spiritualist church service. The first part was very familiar: readings, a talk or sermon, and Protestant type hymns, although with little Christianity or other traditional religious emphasis. The second part was a healing service, when spiritual healers in the congregation came forward to small benches. We were invited to receive a 10 minute healing from one of the volunteers, which I did. The last part was a message service, when an invited medium in the community did four or five short readings of congregants, with their permission. I enjoyed the services.

The last event of weekend three, following a written exam, was our 20 minute readings of two strangers. Our teacher brought in 20 or so friends and community people to be the subjects of student readings. I worried the whole week before that I would produce 40 minutes of silence, which prompted me to do a lot of practicing.

We prepared for our readings by choosing different places in a large hall where we set two chairs facing each other. Then we attempted to quiet our minds before the "customers" arrived.

My first reading was a woman in her early sixties. All we knew were first names, and they were instructed not to volunteer any information. My first impression was that she was involved in a property issue, and that rang no bells. My conscious mind took over, and very little happened after that, although she was very pleasant. I found out afterwards that she was a medium and an artist, who did her readings by sketching and giving the results to her client. I was annoyed that I picked up nothing about art.

My second reading was a woman of about fifty. I got her being a strong business person. That was right, but not what she was interested in exploring. So I turned the dial to relationships and got an impression that she was involved with a strong male figure, with considerable conflict. Underneath the conflict there was some unspoken issue. This seemed to be right on target, and she encouraged me to keep on this track. From that point on, I talked from experience, not from psychic information – from my left brain, I suppose. I told her this, but it didn't matter, and I apparently helped her think through something important to her. Well after the course I reflected that this was not a definitive test of my mediumship, since I know of many women around fifty who have relationship issues.

Since the course, I have watched John Edward, a psychic medium, many times on late night television, and I've read both his books. He is very good at this, and everything I learned shows up in his work, including the admonitions about intention. I also read a short book by Arthur Conan Doyle, written in 1918 and recently republished. Conan Doyle was a physician who wrote the Sherlock Holmes mysteries and a definitive history of Spiritualism after a long personal investigation of the practice of mediums.

My conclusions? Psychic mediums are real. The effective ones are probably quite rare. On a scale of 1 to 10, I would rate my psychic aptitude about 6. With a lot of disciplined work I could perhaps get to 7. The real mediums are around 8 or more to start with. There were two or three in my class, and I respect this most unusual ability.

So, mediumship doesn't look like a promising line of work for me to enter, along with such things as professional sports, oil painting, and rock music. Still, I intend to check in with Leonard from time to time to see what's going on out there.

April, 2003
A Very Brief Tour of The Nonphysical Universe

Excerpts from a presentation to the Philosophical Club of Cleveland

A Hindu sage named Patanjali once wrote about the insights available through diligent practice of meditation: knowledge of past and future; knowledge of past lives; perception of the small, the concealed, the distant; knowledge about the stars and their motions; knowledge of the interior of the body, and so on. That was written in about 400 BCE. His list more or less covers my topics today.

The Scientific Paradigm

The history of science in the Christian era in Europe is almost nonexistent. The Church had the answers. They also had most of the people who could read and write, so it wasn't hard to control. But a few trouble makers surfaced in the 16th and 17th centuries.

One was Copernicus, the Polish astronomer who had some revolutionary ideas about the earth going around the sun. But he also knew which way the wind blew, so he did not release his manuscript until he was dying.

A turning point came in the 17th century when Descartes proposed that the world's knowledge and wisdom should be divided into two parts: matters of natural philosophy (i.e. science) and matters of the spirit (i.e. the Church). Little did the Church know that its authority had started on a long downhill slide, as Bacon, Newton, and the great thinkers of the European enlightenment ran with this new freedom. We can say that science has had a 300 year run. In fact, it has become the principal belief system of the educated Western world, and increasingly now, the Eastern.

Let's put this 300 year period in the context of human history. Humans have exhibited some kind of reflective thinking ability for over 75,000 years. About 2500 years ago there were some lasting philosophical changes as the major world religions began to form, and so on up to the last 300 years of scientific and industrial revolution. I believe we are now undergoing another revolution, this one in our understanding of consciousness. The rest of this presentation suggests some elements of this new revolution.

Today, the overriding scientific paradigm is that the real world is the material or physical world, described remarkably well by contemporary science. Consciousness does not fit in that paradigm; it has been recognized as an anomaly for some time. *Nobody has explained how unconscious matter in our familiar physical world gives rise to consciousness.* So, it's mostly disregarded.

One new paradigm, suggested by physicists such as the late David Bohm, Amit Goswami, and Peter Russell, defines the faculty of consciousness itself as the primary entity, more fundamental than space, time, and matter. Some scientists believe that consciousness is in everything from subatomic particles on up. Although a single cell has a billionth of the richness of our human life experience, there is no evidence that this single cell does not have some form of consciousness.

In the current paradigm, human beings are seen to be assemblies of subatomic particles, separate from one another and from the living and nonliving things around us. There are two important consequences of this paradigm that shape our beliefs.

The first is the notion that we are basically material beings, driven by our chemistry and biology. This tends to give us a material outlook on life – not in the materialistic, greedy sense, but in the value we place on activity in the external physical world as opposed to a more reflective, internal life. It's not likely you would say this about a Buddhist monk.

The second consequence is the belief in separateness, such that we can dispassionately observe the world around us in making judgments or doing experiments. We easily think of "I" and the object "it", and our Western languages support this. However, in many indigenous cultures where the scientific paradigm does not prevail, there is no way in the languages to distinguish "I" and "it", since they are part of the same whole. This is closer to the new paradigm.

Our models are based on the physical universe in which we live, governed by the science of the last 300 years. Yet there exists a very large amount of nonphysical data that doesn't fit the scientific paradigm of space, time, and matter. I'll talk about a few examples today, but it's fair to say that there are centuries of recorded observations and insights, and now over a hundred years of controlled, reproducible experiments demonstrating phenomena that do not fit. Either the data are faulty or the model is incomplete. I'm convinced that the model is the problem.

My background is in applied science, and I retain a strong hope that science can move into these new areas and ideas with an open mind. I should also say that I have one basic belief that really keeps me chipping away at these things. That is, the universe, physical and nonphysical, is logical. That's certainly not provable. It's a belief.

In regard to scientific laws, William James phrased the problem succinctly when he said that in order to test the proposition that all crows are black, all you need is one white crow. Out of all the current explorations of the nonphysical world, I've picked eight to mention today, eight stops on the tour of the nonphysical universe. These are the kind of data that have convinced me that the paradigm should change. These are some of the white crows.

Stops on the Tour

1. Intuition

Intuitive and psychic experiences, along with some elements of dreams, are essentially similar processes. Intuition usually refers to information received when needed, without forethought or preparation. Psychic experiences are usually sought and prepared for, such as prayer healing at a distance, or readings by psychic mediums.

The most common experience is simple intuition. You know when the phone's about to ring before it happens. You may also know who is calling, without caller ID. You sense danger around the curve and you slow down. Or more dramatically, your identical twin or your long-time partner in another city is injured and you feel it simultaneously.

Intuition is associated with the nonphysical part of our world. We call it the universal consciousness, but you might want to think of it as a psychic internet that provides each of us, through our psyches, a direct link to the rest of the world – the nonphysical part – although some of the connections are very, very faint. There's no monthly charge, by the way, for logging on to the psychic internet.

2. Species Consciousness

Earlier, I raised the question how consciousness, specifically human consciousness, could have arisen from unconscious matter. One simple and logical answer is that it has been present from the beginning of time. But let's stick to earth time for now.

For most of the first four billion years of earth's existence, the only living organisms were simple bacteria, one-celled entities with no nucleus. They essentially shaped the surface of our planet. In the course of the next billion years, more complex plants and animals evolved, with humans of some sort appearing 200,000 or 300,000 years ago. Lewis Thomas once suggested that we were invented by the bacteria as taxicabs to carry them around.

I'd like to call your attention to an innovative Greek-American scientist by the name of Elisabet Sahtouris, a post-Darwinian evolutionary biologist. She believes that the history of earth, and the living species on earth, parallel the history of the universe in being *self-organizing*. She uses the term intelligent self-organization, implying some kind of species consciousness. Thus, she disagrees with Darwin followers by rejecting accidents as a primary force behind evolution.

Sahtouris makes a distinction between mature and immature species (bacteria and humans, for example). Mature species that have survived have worked through competition to a point where they cooperate and share – in order to survive. Such activities imply some kind of shared consciousness. Humans have not reached maturity yet, but she sees the growth of the internet as a form of species sharing, and cause for some optimism about the future of our species. Of course, there are plenty of activities in the present world leading to pessimism. But we've only had 300,000 years.

A principal idea in Sahtouris' scheme is that the universe is a living entity, from the spiral galaxies in outer space down to the swirling subatomic particles. She reminds us that ancient bacteria created the first world-wide web in the form of a DNA exchange, cooperatively sharing genetic material and information needed for evolutionary development. She believes that this DNA information exchange could not have resulted from the random forces of nature, but from intelligent self-organization.

3. Remote Viewing

Susan and I have personal experience in remote viewing, a form of perception at a distance, or the psychic retrieval of information about a place distant from the viewer.

Remote viewing is a practice of meditation or quieting the mind, then concentrating on an arbitrary number that is intentionally connected, usually by a photograph or map, to some location in the world. The objective is to bring back definitive information about it, beyond what appears on the photograph or map. The viewer has no information about the location other than the number; only the test supervisor knows that this number designates Mt. Everest, for instance.

The practice of remote viewing was sponsored by the CIA and US Military for 20 years as a means of gathering military intelligence; much of the work was done at the Stanford Research Institute. They had many successes in finding hostages and lost submarines, describing the interior of secret Russian installations, and much more.

Before I went to my first training session in remote viewing, I read some books on the subject and was intrigued. So late one evening I did what I was taught to do – an experiment. I pulled a three-month old *Newsweek* out of a stack, picked an arbitrary page number (28) out of the air, and set the magazine aside without opening it. After a few minutes of quiet meditation, but keeping the page number in mind, I took a blank piece of paper and sketched whatever came into my awareness without attempting any interpretation. There were five images, no words. Then I compared page 28 and my sketches. To my amazement, all five were elements of the photograph on the page. Since then, we attended training and did some practice viewing at home. Some were fairly successful, some not at all. We've not continued the practice in any disciplined way, since our goal is understanding the process, not becoming experts.

4. Spiritualism and the Afterlife

One of the less ordinary psychic practices is that of mediums or spiritualists – people who bring messages from the dead. Since its high point in the late 1800's, mediums have lost most of their following because of many exposed frauds. However, Professor Gary Schwartz at the University of Arizona recently did a careful study of mediums by assembling five American practitioners with the best reputations. He had them independently obtain information from the same deceased persons, and got quite astounding results that were consistent and accurate to a high statistical degree. Many writers have described positive medium experiences.

(See "My Short Life as a Medium", Jan 2002, about my mediumship course at Lilydale.)

5. Distant Healing

Medical practitioners are held in high regard in our culture, as in all human history. So it's no surprise that new findings about prayer healing at a distance have caused much excitement, not only in medical circles. Distant healing is a phenomenon that seems to exhibit nonlocality and transmission of thoughts through the psychic internet.

Larry Dossey is a medical doctor who has written and spoken about this for the last 10 years, especially the beneficial effect of prayer. The studies of special interest are those where the patients do not know they are being prayed for, those doing the praying are a long way distant and they have no personal interaction with the patients. I'll summarize one of the many published studies of distant healing.

Forty AIDS patients in San Francisco were divided into target and control groups. Forty experienced healers around the country took part, from Christian, Jewish, Buddhist, Native American, and shamanic traditions. Each patient was treated by prayer, long distance, by ten different healers, one hour a day for six consecutive days. The patients did not know whether they were in the target or control group. At the end of the study the target group experienced significantly better medical and quality of life outcomes on many measures, including fewer outpatient visits, fewer days of hospitalization, less severe illnesses acquired during the study, and less emotional distress. This was published in 1998 in the *Western Journal of Medicine*.

6. Medical Intuition

(See "My Affair with S", June, 1998, for a recollection of medical intuitive readings by Caroline Myss.)

In 2000, I experienced medical diagnosis myself in a small way. I attended a workshop in New Jersey with a psychic healer. The first exercise was to pair up with someone we did not know and attempt to read each other, following the psychic's instructions. My partner was a woman in her forties. I went through a series of steps to clear my conscious mind and then imagined shining a light through her body in order to note any dark spots. Needless to say, I had very little confidence in the results. I told her I found two dark areas, in her left hip and left foot or ankle. To the amazement of both of us, she said yes and yes. She had recently seen medical professionals for both of those problems, and she did not know of any other current medical problem.

Susan has had positive experience with a local woman who has a high degree of medical intuition, especially about chronic medical problems. Like Caroline Myss, she seems to sense energy fields associated with different parts of the body.

Susan's and my psychic experiences in remote viewing, mediumship, and medical intuition were done on purpose with help from experienced people. For those activities we tried ourselves, it seemed clear that the more we practiced, the easier such exercises would become. The main element of practice is learning to clear our conscious minds out of the way; there are many known ways to do that, from meditation to drugs.

7. Brain Waves and Altered States of Consciousness

The correlation between brain waves and states of consciousness may be the best known connection between scientific measurement and psychic activity. When we dream, meditate, or engage in many types of psychic activity, an EEG device hooked up to our head will show a significant fraction of theta waves of 4 to 8 cycles per second. Right now, unless you are bored and daydreaming, you and I would show a preponderance of beta waves, over 14 cycles per second. In between is alpha, where our ability to learn and absorb is high. The lowest frequency is delta, which we exhibit when deeply asleep.

The altered state of theta brain waves is not all that mysterious. We experience it every day as we fall asleep on our way to deep sleep. This is when we dream. This also seems to be when we gather and process information and guidance that helps us solve ordinary problems.

The correlation between brain waves and states of consciousness has been studied for 30 years. In one line of research started by Robert Monroe, it has been found that by sending audio waves of slightly different frequencies into a subject's two ears, the brain picks up the difference and exhibits increased brain waves of that frequency difference. For example, if audible signals of 200 and 205 cycles per second are sent to earphones, the subject exhibits an increase of brain waves around 5 cycles per second, or theta. Consequently, one can voluntarily enter an altered state rather quickly, and experience the state as if you had gotten there by meditation. This is the basis for some devices on the market for improving relaxation, learning ability, and so forth.

8. Guidance

When we seek guidance through prayers or meditation, or just by sleeping on a problem, where do the answers come from? Is there a Wisdom Central in the universal consciousness, or do we need to search even higher on the ladder? This seems to be a step beyond just considering the universal consciousness to be a psychic internet of information.

In the past 40 years there have been at least two well known cases of guidance in this country, where apparently randomly selected individuals had multiple volumes of thoughtful text channeled through them, in English, ready for publication. One is *A Course in Miracles*, brought to light through two New York psychologists in the 1960's. The other is a series of papers and books channeled through Jane Roberts in Elmira, New York by a being named Seth, also in the sixties. Between them they have sold over a million volumes and have led to study groups around the world. *Miracles* has a strong Christian flavor, and presents an intensive spiritual training program focusing on love and the presence of the divine. Seth discusses transcendence, altered states of consciousness, and different realities.

(See more on Seth in "The Nature of Angels", Jan, 2005.)

Why Bother?

Life is busy enough. Why should I spend time trying to fathom the nonphysical world, if there is such a thing? Good question. I'd like to conclude with some thoughts from a scientist, philosopher, and economist named Chris Thomson.

Like many others in the field of consciousness, he speaks of the metaparadigm we are living in, 20th century science. The basic claims of this paradigm are that the physical world is primary, everything can be explained in terms of the physical, and there is probably no greater intelligence than ours.

These beliefs have consequences. One is the predominance of material values. Second is a tendency to ignore other ways of knowing such as intuition or telepathy. Third is a disregard for important content beyond current scientific boundaries.

His prescription is to value all forms of knowing, strive to develop the less familiar ways, and integrate them into your life. Not surprisingly, listen to your common sense. The use of all forms of knowing can also guide the way we practice science, health, and education. The result will be a fuller engagement with the whole world, leading to more open-mindedness, less exploitation of nature and people, and a richer life.

The Nature of Angels

Presented to the Philosophical Club of Cleveland

Readings

First, three readings about angels or spirit beings.

Hildegard of Bingen (11th Century): According to their nature, angels are invisible, but they take their bodies from the atmosphere, and appear visible in the human form to those they are sent to as messengers. They also adopt other human habits. They do not speak to humans with angelic tongues, but instead with words that can be understood.

St. Thomas Aquinas (13th Century): Angels do not need bodies for their own sake but for ours.

Emanuel Swedenborg (18th Century): By spirits, human beings have communication with the world of spirits, and through angels with heaven. Without these communications, people could not live at all. Our life entirely depends on this conjunction, so that if the spirits and angels were to withdraw, we would instantly perish.

One more reading, this one in the words of an apparent spirit being. It's reported by *Jane Roberts*, in 1970 in "The Seth Material". Seth, a channeled entity, is speaking about consciousness through Jane Roberts in a session on July 6, 1964.

Chemicals themselves will not give rise to consciousness or life. Your scientists will have to face the fact that consciousness comes first and evolves its own form... All the cells in the body have a separate consciousness. There is a conscious cooperation between the cells in all the organs, and between the organs themselves... Molecules and atoms and even smaller particles have a condensed consciousness. They form into cells and form an individual cellular consciousness. This combination results in a consciousness that is capable of much more experience and fulfillment than would be possible for the isolated atom or molecule alone. This goes on ad infinitum... to form the physical body mechanism. Even the lowest particle retains its individuality and its abilities, through this cooperation, are multiplied a millionfold.

Introduction

Angels have been dismissed by most Western scientific and religious authorities since the scientific revolution some 300 years ago. That includes the modern branches of the Roman Catholic Church which, in medieval times, saw angels as the way God governed the world. So, angels are currently out. They're spiritually incorrect.

And yet... a Time Magazine survey in the 1990's found that two thirds of Americans believed in the existence of angels, and a surprising one third felt their presence in their lives. It's hard to throw out all that data.

A tragic newspaper story four years ago got my attention. Six teenagers lost their lives in an automobile accident near Medina, Ohio in December, 2000. One 14 year old girl named Katie survived. A month later she was interviewed when leaving the hospital. She said she saw *ladies in pretty white robes* touch everyone but her, moments after the accident. The story put quotation marks around not only Katie's remarks, but later around the word *angels*, when relating how the vision comforted the families. Quotation marks or not, I have no question she saw what she said she saw.

In the following sections, I'll summarize traditional and individual concepts about angels, and channeled beings such as "Seth". Then some ideas about different levels of consciousness that might (someday) explain the source of angelic or channeled communication.

Traditional Views

Although we most easily may connect angels with traditional Christianity, all cultures have contained beliefs in spirits or non-physical beings beyond human life experiences; the similarities are much greater than the differences. Spirits are common in Jewish and Muslim traditions, and they abound in Eastern religions and primitive cultures. A case can be made that many of the spirits or gods of polytheistic religions were assimilated into the monotheistic religions as angels.

Medieval scholars, with a mindset much like modern scientists, were drawn to classification and ranking of angels as to their importance in God's scheme. The most popular number was nine types of angels, usually arranged in three levels of seniority. This was first written down by Dionysius the Areopagite in the 5th century. He lived in Syria and influenced centuries of theologians, including St. Thomas Aquinas in the 13th century. Another theologian of great influence was Hildegard of Bingen in the 11th century. Angels were an important part of her cosmology, although she preferred a circular organization instead of a hierarchical one. Those of you who study the differences between males and females are probably nodding in agreement.

There is a significant difference between the visions of scholars such as these three and the experiences of millions of contemporary Americans. The scholars were concerned with the overall organization of the universe as they knew it and the mechanism for transmission of God's will to humans. Angels were viewed as messengers and part of the cosmic government structure. In contrast, individuals usually feel a personal guidance or protection.

I want to be cautious in talking about the governing function. Perhaps I should say "suggesting" instead. In all traditions there is a common notion of free will for humans. That's why the idea of bad or shadow angels is important. We receive good, constructive suggestions as well as bad temptations, as did Dr. Faust in the legend. We must choose.

Individual Experiences

Most personal experiences of angels are about protection from injury or death in exceptional circumstances, attributed to the intervention of guardian angels. The most common experience is an intuitive message or feeling to duck just before a bullet comes our way, or to apply the brakes just before another car pulls into our path. It's reasonable to call these things good luck, and leave it at that... whatever you mean by good luck.

However, a smaller, but still very large number of people actually have experienced the presence of a spirit being, and some have had conversations with these beings. People who have such encounters often have no personal religious practice. That is, the experience of angels is spiritual, not religious. It's not associated with beliefs.

Most of the relevant research studies of experiences with angels or spirit beings in the last forty years have been about near-death experiences. There are hundreds of books and papers on this subject. These accounts are about the experiences of people who have survived after their heart has stopped for several minutes.

Perhaps the most respected person in our time to record these experiences is the late Elisabeth Kubler Ross, psychiatrist and author of *On Death and Dying*, whose life work was to assist the dying, over 20,000 individuals. Writing about terminally ill patients, she said, "All of these patients have experienced a floating out of their physical bodies, associated with a great sense of peace and wholeness. Most were aware of another person who helped them in their transition to another plane of existence." In an interview in 1992, she summarized her experience of death. "I don't believe. I know. I know that life does not stop at death. That's all. It is not a question of believing something but of knowing."

A few people in recorded history have claimed to have extensive contact with angels beyond occasional visions during crises or near-death experiences. The clear winner for duration was Emanuel Swedenborg, who had daily conversations with angels the last 27 years of his life, which ended in 1772. He carefully recorded these conversations. Swedenborg was far from a lonely outsider. In fact, he was one of the towering geniuses of the European enlightenment: a mining engineer who wrote the first major text on mineralogy, a member of the Swedish parliament, a medical researcher, a theologian, and writer of dozens of books. Along the way, he designed an aircraft and machines for his country's military. He is revered by members of the Christian sect known as Swedenborgians to this day.

Swedenborg believed, through his conversations with angels, that we are spirits with bodies while on earth. After death, our spirits continue. He also taught that spirits exist in communities of similar values. They have busy existences, and are not always hovering about living people. They are particularly active with newborn children and at the time of death, and are available for guidance when asked. An important part of his message is the notion of free will – that we are continually required to make choices during life on earth. But our physical life is just one layer of our existence.

Many others have reported conversations with angels, though not as long as Swedenborg's 27 years. Perhaps the most celebrated is Joan of Arc, who had two years of conversations with angels before her untimely end. She was advised to enter battle to save France in 1429, and she proceeded to do just that, at 17 years old.

Seth

One way people have experienced communications from spirit beings is through channeling, a popular source of instructional texts in the last fifty years. No doubt, some of the accounts are fabrications, at least in part. They are part of the so-called "New Age" phenomena that include a lot of silliness along with the profound. That is, it is both spiritual and commercial, like much of traditional religion.

Channeling became a publishing success with two special works of 1960's America: *A Course in Miracles*, and the *Seth* books. Both are claimed to be channeled through the unlikely authors from spirit beings. The Course in Miracles has a strong Christian flavor, while the Seth books have a more scientific viewpoint. These books have sold millions of copies and are widely studied around the world. Whether or not we should pay attention to these sources, or even the Gospels for that matter, seems to come down to this. If there are spirit beings among us, why would they not see that a book of guidance is written, if it is needed? I quoted Seth on consciousness at the beginning of this talk, and will make a few comments about him.

Seth is the name of a nonphysical being that was channeled in the 1960's and 70's in Elmira, New York by a young woman named

Jane Roberts, a poet and writer. Twice a week, for fifteen years, Seth spoke through Jane, while she was in a deep trance, or altered state of consciousness, and her husband wrote it all down. In many cases, other people attended the sessions, and some are recorded on audio tape and video. This led to 50 volumes of Seth material that are the basis of study groups around the world to this day. Over three million copies of the Seth books have been sold. The material is quite remarkable.

Seth describes himself as a spirit entity with a teaching mission. He has lived on the earth plane in a number of incarnations, male and female. He speaks of consciousness, scientific theories, reincarnation, physical and psychological health, planes of existence, the meaning of time in different worlds, and hundreds of other subjects. He speaks in detail of the "inner self" of our personalities that exists apart from our physical existence on the earth plane. In many ways, he outlined concepts in the 1960's that have become central to the extension of quantum physics into consciousness in the 1980's. He frequently stressed that consciousness characterizes the larger world, and that our physical world is one of many projections of consciousness into physical reality. Norman Friedman, a contemporary physicist, has written of the parallels between Seth teachings and quantum physics.

Quantum Physics

Before I attempt to put angels in a modern framework, I want to say a few words about extensions of quantum physics into the nonphysical world.

Quantum physics, as developed in the 20th century, is a remarkable intellectual endeavor. It started as a way to explain certain experiments indicating that fundamental units of matter and energy could be treated either as particles or waves, depending on the observer and the experiment. The resulting mathematical formulation is known as the wave equation. This essentially gives the probabilities of events yet to occur. The terminology is that the probabilities collapse into one actual event, but only when there is an observer.

The basic concept of quantum physics is well supported by experiment. For some time, physicists worked only with events on the scale of electrons and the simplest atom, hydrogen. The last fifty years have seen many extensions of the basic idea and many experiments. Inevitably some theoreticians have applied the ideas to the larger world, leading to such notions as parallel universes where certain probable events are played out in existences other than our familiar physical universe.

These last ideas are not mainstream, but they are creeping in, as theoretical physicists are essentially asking religious questions about nonphysical reality. There is a growing sense in some quarters that the larger universe, including the physical one, is inherently mathematical. That idea is not new, as the ancient Greek philosophers were inclined that way.

As stated before, a few physicists have taken a considerable leap by postulating that the fundamental essence of the universe is consciousness. Our physical world is simply one manifestation of consciousness, essentially a projection on the physical plane of a larger, nonphysical entity. Seth used the analogy of the condensation of one's breath on a cold window pane to describe our familiar physical world.

The exciting prospect is that these theories may eventually be testable. We are approaching a time when, against all expectations, theology may finally have a scientific basis. The two worlds of Descartes may eventually become one.

Working Models of Reality

Traditional religions offer well-defined models of reality based mostly on ancient texts. Liberal religions, where I live, and the nonreligious, tend to reject traditional faith approaches as nonscientific, historically outdated, and authoritarian. We accept the human wisdom of figures such as Jesus, for example, because his teachings about behavior, except for the divine part, hold up well in the light of experience. We are likely to say that Jesus was exceptionally wise, just as Karl Jung and Einstein were exceptional. Strictly speaking, however, some of us might be uncomfortable with Jung's belief in a collective unconscious, or Einstein's belief, not in a personal God, but in a spirit manifested in the laws of the universe.

So we, i.e. the liberal religionists and the nonreligious, accept the teachings of Jesus but not his God-centered model of reality – the source he claimed for the teachings. But what is our model? The central belief system of the modern educated world is physical science, whether or not we have much scientific training.

But what about religious questions? Contemporary science provides little basis for answering questions such as how the universe is organized beyond what our telescopes tell us, why are we born only to die, what is our purpose on earth, and on what basis should we make ethical choices about life and death. These eternal questions simply will not go away. I believe that science – that is, a rational approach to life – will eventually open these persistent questions to our understanding. But not the science of today.

Since I've climbed out on a limb, I might as well go a bit further and outline my working model of reality. To start, I believe that our familiar physical world, well described by contemporary science, is part of a much larger world which we call the nonphysical universe, mostly rejected by today's scientists. Yet, there is substantial evidence of this nonphysical world in phenomena ranging from simple intuition to controlled laboratory experiments. In between are volumes of experiential and anecdotal accounts of interactions between the physical and nonphysical realms. Many accounts are intrinsic to the ancient wisdom traditions. In the next two brief sections, I will comment on the notions of holarchies and parallel universes.

Holarchies

One model of the universe that accounts for much of the nonphysical data is the idea of holarchies, a word popularized by the philosopher Ken Wilber. Holarchies are systems that are nested within higher level systems like Russian dolls, each held together and energized by some form of consciousness, for lack of a better word. A holarchy is more than the sum of its parts by virtue of its consciousness. One can think of consciousness as a glue or energy that binds the system together.

A human being is a holarchy that is composed of smaller and simpler systems known as organs and cells. In turn, cells have components that are even simpler, and so on down through molecules and atoms and beyond. A general oversight is provided by the human brain, but it is neither continuous nor dominant. For example, cells know how to obtain nutrients and expel waste without the brain getting involved in the details. The brain becomes involved when the whole system requires it. The language of communication, as far as we know, is through chemical messengers such as hormones, and electrical impulses. Our brains rely on the subsystems knowing what to do in normal operation, and it is unlikely that brains attempt to communicate directly with atoms within the cells. In fact, they probably don't have a suitable language to do so.

Going up the ladder of the physical universe, human families, clans, and belief groups form larger holarchies that communicate in ways beyond simple language. For instance, at the family level, it is well known that identical twins, mothers and children, or long-time partners sometimes obtain intuitive and immediate messages over great distances when one is injured. Jung's concept of the collective unconscious extends this idea to humankind in general. Biologist Rupert Sheldrake speaks of morphic fields that connect us, and other living beings, in ways that allow us to develop our species characteristics and inter-communication.

Higher on the ladder of physical complexity, we humans receive a variety of communications from our environment and the planet as a whole in language as familiar as weather changes or as rare as earthquakes and tsunamis. Sometimes we pay attention, and sometimes we don't. We certainly get strong messages when our actions endanger the health of our environment and planet. Note that we do not need to invoke the idea of a God of the entire universe to pay attention to our ecosystems.

What about holarchies greater than planet earth? Our solar system, our galaxy, and the universe beyond? If you agree with the scheme so far, it is logical that there are higher and higher levels of consciousness with the ability to communicate within these levels, but probably with very limited ability to speak directly to humans, just as we cannot speak directly to the atoms in our bodies.

Parallel universes

The idea of holarchies structuring our physical universe, with multiple levels of consciousness, can explain a lot of the nonphysical data available to us. It is an attractive scheme for explaining nonphysical interactions among humans, or between humans and animals, or between humans and the environment. But it falls short of explaining things such as communications from the afterlife or reincarnation, to name just two well-studied phenomena. In order to delve into these things, we need to consider the idea of parallel universes, where our familiar physical plane is just one of many universes existing together.

Parallel universes are a tough subject, to be sure. We live and act in a physical universe and have no capacity other than inference and speculation as to any others. Our words limit us. But we keep trying. The religions of the world attempt to do this by invoking some concept of God or Gods. These traditional religious schemes are rooted in earlier times, before much, if any, of the relevant scientific data was known. Also, they tend to be anthropomorphic, projecting human characteristics onto the deities. In a similar way, perhaps, simple cells sense that they are simply part of a larger group of cells instead of something as complex as the human body with a much more elaborate consciousness. That is, we humans naturally picture the universe as human-like, while cells may picture it as cell-like.

What about interventions in our physical world from other sources of consciousness in the nonphysical universe? I believe that angels might be seen as a form of intervention that could make sense to many humans, whether their human-like form was imposed from the outside or from our own minds. Spectacular interventions from nonphysical sources occur infrequently, perhaps when most needed. These include unexplainable miracles and channeled texts, for example. Maybe the resurrection of Jesus was such an intervention. And why not? The resurrection story certainly underlined his important teachings, which have become codified in the human institution of Christianity.

Summary

I certainly am not able to say there are beings known as spirits or angels who have human forms. However, millions of people have received important nonphysical communications in languages they understand, and they often have experienced a being with a more-or-less human form. Whether the form is created by their minds or by the nonphysical communication source is a minor issue. The major issue is the communication itself.

I do believe there are higher – and lower – levels of consciousness than our own. This seems to be a consistent and simple explanation for numerous observations and human experiences – data that just don't fit in the current scientific paradigm of space, time, and matter. These experiences include spectacular interventions as well as simple, everyday intuitive information.

The higher levels of consciousness intervene in our affairs from time to time through some means of communication we can understand, similar to the brain's oversight of the organs in our bodies. The traditional concept of angels or spirit beings as messengers fits this model.

The communications arrive when needed, sometimes to protect us, sometimes to heal or teach us. They are transmitted intuitively for the most part. In much rarer cases, perhaps at times of greatest need, the nonphysical communications come in more specific and unusual forms: channeled texts, visual apparitions, or so-called miracles.

These higher levels of consciousness do not intervene most of the time for most of us, and we can choose to pay attention or disregard them. Their presence does not imply a fatalistic character to life on earth. Far from it. All traditions and our human experience teach that we must continually make choices. Some choices may be better informed than others if we pay attention to our intuition. To our common sense.

References

Matthew Fox and Rupert Sheldrake, "The Physics of Angels" (1996)

Pierre Jovanovic, "An Inquiry into the Existence of Guardian Angels" (1993)

Robert Kirven, "Angels in Action: What Swedenborg Saw and Heard" (1994)

October, 2005

Our Brains Protect Us

Brains, it is reported, have the ability to change certain memories. The reasoning is that they protect us from current negative effects that can keep us from functioning in the real, physical world. Some psychotherapy patients work very hard to recall such memories in order to cope with present circumstances.

In our excursions into the paranormal world, we have found a kind of beginner's luck at work. The first time we try something new, it often works as advertised. Subsequent attempts are not as fruitful. I found this in remote viewing and medical intuition. Some energy healers have said, with a smile, that a healer often gets three "free" healings before running into trouble. Is this the protective brain doing its thing?

Practitioners of psychic behavior warn the new student about this phenomenon. Whether remote viewing, recalling dreams, or attempting to pick up and pin down impressions in a reading, as in psychic mediumship, the instruction is to hold on to your very first impressions. These are most likely to be the most accurate. Apparently the brain wakes up and soon organizes incoming information into already known categories. Only with practice can you resist this brain exercise and allow the new information to make its way to the conscious mind.

The brain is reluctant to let us absorb or experience data that does not fit what we already know.

What about people who regularly think "out of the box?" Inventors of things or ideas, scientific explorers, creative artists? Sometimes the new ideas are intelligent syntheses of information and thought processes previously learned. But other times, the creator does actually take a turn in his or her mind into new territory. Often, even the traveler cannot be sure which route was taken.

A useful model is that our conscious minds have a small aperture to the unconscious, or more generally, to the nonphysical world of intuitive information. The aperture size varies with individuals, and its size is probably conditioned by evolution. Too large an aperture could be associated with psychological instability, an inability to deal with day-to-day functioning in the real, physical world. Perhaps some visionaries and great artists are in this category. Many have been known to do rather poorly with daily living. In an extreme case, you might find an idiot savant – someone barely functioning but able to carry out incredible mental feats.

Too small an aperture could also be life threatening, if you accept that regular use of intuitive information is essential to full and healthy living. Here are the people who are reluctant to rely on their "gut feeling" that a situation is dangerous or likely to end in failure or disaster. Thus evolution appears to give most of us a small, but not too large, ability to reach into the unconscious, the world of intuitive information.

But wouldn't it be nice to be able to access this world when it is appropriate? Many people do so, in both unintentional and intentional ways. The natural practice of intuitive access goes back to prerecorded history. In fact, some studies of primitive peoples around the world have shown that it may be more common in them than in modern educated people. It shows up in sixth-sense intuition of people who live in the wild about dangers from predatory animals, enemies, and nature. A recent, widely replicated study by Rupert Sheldrake, the biologist, demonstrates that we all seem to have some ability to sense when we are stared at from behind our heads. That may not be an important survival skill in modern city life, but it certainly is out in the jungle.

Intentional practices that have the effect of widening the aperture take many forms. All of these involve creating for oneself an altered state of consciousness. The resultant state is marked by the increased prevalence of theta brain waves of 4-8 cycles per second on an EEG scan. (See "A Very Brief Tour of the Nonphysical Universe", April, 2003, for more detail.)

The theta state is known from ancient times as a goal of deep meditation. It also can be brought about by certain drugs such as LSD. One problem with drugs, aside from dangerous side effects, is that one may experience a wild induced ride but not be able to absorb insights or information that are useful back in normal life.

A practice similar to meditation is guided imagery, where one minimizes thoughts and influences from the surroundings and concentrates on, say, a peaceful scene. Like meditation, the goal is to clear the conscious mind out of the way, as much as possible, in order to open access to intuitive information.

The use of meditation or imagery to clear the conscious mind and enter an altered state is a discipline used by most people who practice psychic phenomena. It is easier for some than others. But it is available to all who want to make better use of their natural capacity to gain access to the intuitive information that exists in the world. However, it would be a poor idea to practice it while crossing a busy street. Our brains work very hard to avoid such a foolish mistake.

November, 2005
Tuning In To Intuition

In 2001 I wrote "The Radio Analogy" which included some thoughts about tuning into the nonphysical world. These notes continue the subject. The idea is that the transmittal of intuitive information has some of the characteristics of wave propagation, but differs in other ways from what we know about waves.

Although intuitive information transfer continues to be controversial among traditional scientists, I have no doubt that it exists in many forms. We know that it occurs; we don't know how it occurs. Among human beings, some of its forms are telepathy, remote viewing, the sense of being stared at, and perceptions between well-bonded people such as identical twins or mothers and children. Within animal species, some form of nonphysical communication appears to occur in flocks of birds, schools of fish, and even insect populations. Between humans and animals, it occurs between pets and their masters. All these things are well documented, many by carefully conducted experiments.

Less well documented, and far more controversial, are communications between humans and spirit beings such as psychic mediumship or the revelations of angels. Even more speculative is the possibility of some kind of conscious communication among inorganic materials and fundamental physical units at the atomic level.

The transmittal of energy and information by waves is a fundamental characteristic of our physical world. Waves have frequencies, wave lengths, and amplitudes. There are sound waves, fluid waves, mechanical waves, and the vibration of solid materials. Einstein predicted the existence of gravity waves, and there are experiments in progress around the world to attempt to pin these down. We all know that countless electromagnetic waves surround us, the basis for most of the modern industrial world. This was unknown until the late 1800's, and still is a mystery to most of us. You can describe them mathematically if you have studied physics.

What makes electromagnetism so useful is the phenomenon of resonance, which makes possible the act of tuning. A radio receiver reacts to set frequencies based on the mechanics of the receiver materials, solid crystals in the original radio concept. When the receiver's natural frequency is the same as the transmitter's, a resonance occurs at the receiver, and the information on the radio wave is absorbed, amplified, and converted to sound waves.

Resonance also occurs in strictly mechanical systems such as a suspension bridge. If externally caused vibrations, say from wind or traffic, match the natural frequency of the bridge, the whole structure starts vibrating, with some famous destructive results.

Tuning appears to apply to transmission of intuitive information. Whether the brain is the actual receiver or not, it certainly is involved in the processing of intuitive information received by humans. Perhaps it acts only as the amplifier system. Like a radio, the brain acts as if it can only pick up certain frequencies but not others. For example, our long-term memories may be a case of information channels specific to each of us, not available to other brains. To me, this is a better description of memory than assuming that all that information is carried around inside our heads. I find it hard to believe that the words and notes of a song I heard 50 years ago are stored in my head. What I think is stored is an ability to gain access to that information with the right switch. The musical information is stored elsewhere in the universe.

Consider the identical-twin phenomenon, whereby one twin instantly knows the other is in danger even if separated by hundreds of miles. The information transferred is a feeling that we describe as an emotional response. It has some kind of energy content, for it causes action in the receiver. We can begin to accept such intuitive transfer by saying there is some natural frequency between the twins. But what is the nature of the carrier wave?

Many researchers have attempted to find a part of the electromagnetic spectrum to account for transmissions of this type. Much of the research was done as part of remote viewing programs sponsored by the US and USSR governments. As far as I know, this line of investigation has failed to explain the basis of remote viewing. Two features of electromagnetic waves were found not to apply. One is the distance effect wherein the strength of waves decreases with distance. The other is the blockage of electromagnetic waves by Faraday cages, essentially metal cages that stop the waves. In intuitive transmission, there appears to be no distance effect and it is not stopped by Faraday cages.

So, the transmission of intuitive information seems to have some characteristics like electromagnetic wave propagation such as resonance, tuning, and energy content, but not others such as the distance effect and blockage by Faraday cages.

One area of considerable research is the nature of DNA, and the possibility of DNA itself being some sort of transmitter and receiver. This line of thought is consistent with certain human-to-human communication between close family members. However, it would not explain communication between non-related individuals. I believe there may be a yet undiscovered spectrum of consciousness waves and frequencies. Perhaps DNA research will help lead to an answer.

One interesting line of investigation could be to focus on tuning. An elementary form of tuning is employed in two kinds of psychic practice that are familiar to me, remote viewing and psychic reading. That is the mental checklist. After the viewer or reader enters an altered state of consciousness, for example through meditation, he or she proceeds through categories of information in order to pick up pieces of information. A remote viewer, searching for an unknown object or location, is taught to scan through characteristics such as color, texture, and shape while looking for impressions. A psychic reader searches for information about a person by focusing, in turn, on relationships, health, career or travel. If we could find better, more reliable and reproducible ways to tune into intuitive channels, a consciousness wave theory would begin to have some support. I expect this to happen.

If you find some agreement with these notes, you could say we are on the same wave length.

January, 2006
Why Behave Morally?
A Sermon at the First Unitarian Church of Cleveland

Readings

Most of what I really need to know about how to live and what to do and how to be I learned in kindergarten. Wisdom was not at the top of the graduate school mountain, but there in the sand pile at Sunday school. These are the things I learned:

Share everything.
Play fair.
Don't hit people.
Put things back where you found them.
Clean up your own mess.
Don't take things that aren't yours.
Say you're sorry when you hurt somebody.
Wash your hands before you eat.
Flush.
Warm cookies and cold milk are good for you.
Live a balanced life – learn some and think some and draw and paint and sing and dance and play and work every day some.
Take a nap every afternoon.

When you go out into the world, watch out for traffic, hold hands and stick together.

Be aware of wonder.

- Robert Fulghum (Unitarian Minister and writer), "All I Really Need to Know I Learned in Kindergarten", 1986.

In a sense, religious beliefs are working hypotheses – tested, judged, and validated by the experiences of individuals and societies over time. This method is much like the scientific process, even though it is usually more difficult for us to make convincing religious deductions. Of course, the problems of religion are often more complicated and harder to control for than are scientific theories, and there are quantitative differences that may obscure the logical similarities between the two disciplines. Yet clearly, certain aspects of natural science and social science are very much like religion, relying more on experience and observation than easily reproducible experiments.

But what of the concept of "proof"? Certainly, many would argue that proofs give scientific ideas a kind of absolutism and universalism that religion lacks. In truth, however, we can never prove anything completely. Even scientifically and mathematically, we can never be absolutely sure our conclusions are correct. Our science is based on postulates, or assumptions, which, like faith, we may believe in firmly, but cannot prove absolutely.

As long as our scientific ideas and religious understandings continue to match our experience, both realms will continue to enjoy a substantial degree of acceptable validity. Yes, science and religion emphasize somewhat different areas of our lives, but ultimately, they both deal with the same subjects: ourselves and the universe around us. When we look at the real nature of each, the two disciplines are not so distinguishable, and as we understand each more fully, they will overlap more and more. Eventually, as we progress in our understanding, they will converge. Science and religion are merely two ways of looking at life and the universe; it follows that, in the long run, they will see the same things.

- Charles Townes (Nobel Laureate in Physics, 1964), "Marriage of Two Minds", presented at Queens College, Cambridge, England, Summer 2005.

Sermon

In the last two years I was one of the eighth grade teachers here at the church. I enjoyed this experience very much. These 13 year olds are very busy people. Their families value education, and some of the kids are very good students. They are involved in sports programs. They take lessons in music and other outside activities. They are loyal to their friends, fond of their pets, and appreciative of their families. Teen-age rebellion has not yet taken over, but it's on the horizon.

There are many surprises when working with 8th graders. I'll give one example. One day I posed a problem to the class of eight or nine kids. You come across a wallet or purse in a mall; it contains cash and identification. What do you do with it? To my surprise, all of them present that day would keep some or all of the cash.

Sometime later, after I recovered, I found myself thinking about moral development, a phrase that seems to come from another era. Books about manners and etiquette. Boys sent away to military boarding schools to get straightened out. Discreet Sunday afternoon visits from the minister. After a bit of refresher reading, I was reminded that kids progress through five or six stages of moral development. Young children do best with clear rules of behavior. As they interact with other kids, they learn to make judgments based on fairness and agreements. Then they begin to be exposed to conventional morality. Finally, they start thinking in terms of principles instead of rules. That is, *why* should they behave in a socially acceptable manner?

The small group of 13 year olds that day did not seem to be at the principles stage yet. Maybe that's normal. They have heard *how* to behave for years. The more interesting question is *why* they should behave according to conventional rules of conduct. That's my topic.

I'm glad they didn't ask me *why* at the time, because I would have fumbled around for an answer. Because God made the rules clear? I haven't believed that for a long time. Because they would gain adult approval? Sounds like a guilt trip. Because the rules support the common good? Who says so, and what about their own good? Because they will be happier? Not too convincing. They only need to look around to see that lots of people seem to do quite well living by other moral codes. Looking out for number one. Winning at all costs. Maximizing personal pleasure. Accumulating the most toys.

This simple question, *why*, brings up some clear disagreements in our culture, even among people of good character. If you ask a fundamentalist Christian and a secular humanist to define moral development, you would get similar short answers. Both would emphasize raising children with a sense of right and wrong, with guidelines for behavior in a complex world of good and evil. They both would mention character traits such as honesty and hard work, and both would cite the golden rule.

Longer answers would reveal the philosophical differences. The Christian would talk about God's instructions as transmitted through the Bible and the teachings of Jesus. The promise of heaven for the faithful would be brought up, as would the Ten Commandments.

The humanist would refer to human nature and history, to heroic figures and exemplary common people, and to time-tested principles for healthy and constructive living. He or she would speak of continuing improvement of the global community through the use of science and knowledge.

I am happy to have friends around both philosophical poles, although I'm much closer to the secularist side. The traditional idea of God in Christianity neither appeals to me nor fits with what I know. Yet I'm uneasy that the secular arguments are based on a very weak "why", on a relative approach to moral issues that is scorned by the religious faithful.

It seems to me that moral principles necessarily are derived from a mature understanding of the nature of the world. Then we do our best to pass on this understanding to the kids. In this church we have the luxury of discussing it and arguing about it. However, large numbers of young people are exposed neither to the doctrines of traditional religion nor to the lessons of humanism. They just grow up, picking up morality where they can, mostly from peers, television, the internet, and pop music. Parents, relatives, and schoolteachers are left to fill in the gaps.

Kids develop a moral sense, one way or another. They are works in progress at age 13. The experts on moral development say they need to be introduced to principles around this time, perhaps earlier. But what principles? Let's take one more look at religion and secularism.

In this church community, we reject traditional religious principles for many reasons. Perhaps the primary one is that they were devised by men with earthly agendas, political and economic, as well as spiritual. They were developed in a pre-scientific age and include many assertions that have been proven wrong. Yet, there are many enduring truths between the doctrines and dogma. And many superior human beings stand out in religious history. What doesn't satisfy the liberal religious mind is the concept that God revealed truth to humankind and requires us to worship him, or else. As a result, few of us in this church accept the idea of God as traditionally defined.

On the secularist side, we are enamored with human progress, focusing on behaviors, policies, and good works that improve life for all people. We emphasize the dignity of the individual. We see betterment of life on earth as the goal, knowledge and reason as the routes to that goal. The truly secular believe that's all there is, all that we can possibly know. We are obligated to make the best of it, although I'm not sure why. Among strict humanists, there is no God, no supernatural structure, no guidance from any source other than our own minds and collective experience. If there is a core philosophy that joins modern humanists and other secularists, it is contemporary science.

Let's get back to "why" – Why behave according to a moral code? In short, traditional religionists would say that principles of moral behavior have been laid out by God, through ancient prophets and modern-day interpreters. Secularists would say that principles are evident from history, psychology, science, and pursuit of the common good. Both sides believe that principles of morality must be based on their world views, which are very different.

Not surprisingly, most of the ordinary behaviors consistent with these principles are similar. As Robert Fulghum has written, he learned many important ones in kindergarten. One would think that the two sides could be reconciled. In fact, that is the message of Charles Townes in the excerpt I read earlier. He has been saying that for over fifty years, and he has received much criticism from both the religious and scientific sides. As a culture, we still are strongly influenced by the position laid down by Descartes about 400 years ago – that science and religion are, by definition, totally separate and distinct ways of viewing the world, and will always be so.

I submit that there is a body of investigation going on that may bring these opposing ideas together. It's often called consciousness studies. It's guided by scientific reasoning and research but is not yet embraced by most contemporary scientists. It's partly objective, partly speculative, and it is gaining momentum. It is people from many disciplines looking at hard evidence as well as human experience in order to develop a new understanding of the larger universe in which we live.

It's worthwhile to pause and ask what good can come from studying consciousness? Why bother? How would it change our lives? I see at least two consequences. First, a deeper knowledge of consciousness – that is, how we are connected – can support and guide the way we deal with each other and make decisions. In short, our notions of morality. In the long run, it can prepare humans to be better, more knowledgeable participants in the larger universe. Second, this knowledge can eventually bring the traditional religions together with the secularists. I don't expect either of these outcomes to happen in my lifetime. Still, I would not be surprised if departments of consciousness studies start appearing at universities during the lifetimes of my grandchildren.

With my science and engineering background, I like to use the word "model" to describe this effort. Those who investigate the nature of the universe are contributing to a working model of reality. It will always be incomplete. It will always be in progress.

So, what are some of the possible elements of a new understanding of consciousness, a new model of the universe? I'll try to summarize three general ideas, but I don't have time to back them up with the evidence that appeals to me.

Connectedness. Our familiar world, described very well by Newtonian physics, is just part of a larger one. Some use the phrase "parallel universes". A few quantum physicists know what they mean by that, but it's still mostly a mathematical concept. Other investigators like the concept of a holographic universe, also more theoretical than experimentally defined. One deduction from the parallel-universe model is that we individual human beings are projections, on the physical plane, of larger entities that exist in other planes of existence.

There seem to be connections, or interventions, between one plane and another in the parallel universes. In our familiar plane of existence, some spectacular interventions are called miracles by the faithful. There are ordinary interventions too, as common as intuitive flashes, new thoughts coming in dreams, or unexplained healings. None of these interventions are at odds with free will, for we can and do disregard most of them.

As our seventh Unitarian-Universalist principle states, we are truly interconnected in a web of life, far more than the casual exchange of carbon, hydrogen, and oxygen atoms that we have been carrying out the last 40 minutes. My guess is that DNA research will someday shed light on part of the mechanism. A few investigators think that DNA itself acts as a transmitter and receiver of information, but not through electromagnetic waves. Some of the clearest examples of this connectedness are feelings between closely bonded family members.

Cooperation. Living organisms other than human beings have some sort of consciousness, from animals down to one-celled bacteria. They don't have the gift of communication as we understand it, so it is hard for us to fathom. The consciousness of species is reflected in the cooperation we see throughout nature, among schools of fish or flocks of birds, or even among the bacteria that colonized this planet for its first three billion years or so.

I like the notion of holarchies associated with the philosopher Ken Wilber. In this model of cooperation, each system or holarchy, such as a human being, is more than the sum of its parts by virtue of consciousness. Holarchies may be thought of as nested systems, like Russian dolls. For example, in the human body, organs and cells are progressively smaller holarchies, or sub-systems. They know how to function without continual supervision by the brain. Cells know how to absorb nutrients and expel wastes. They cooperate with each other under a wide variety of stressful conditions, without the brain's involvement.

Continuity. If we define life as a form of consciousness, it may not be extinguished when our bodies die. Consider that the light of long-dead stars still moves through the physical universe, and will continue *ad infinitum*. Similarly, the energies connected with our minds, such as thoughts, emotions, and memories, remain in the universe, perhaps as quanta of energy. There is continuity to existence that neither begins at birth nor ends at death.

Some people have extraordinary abilities to perceive things the rest of us cannot, such as energy fields, colored auras, medical insights, even thoughts and dreams of other people. I know some of you in this congregation have some of these intuitive abilities, including one of the kids who passed through my 8th grade class.

There are two features of extrasensory perception that I think belong in this summary of continuity. In many demonstrated cases involving intuitive communication between two parties, the two need not be physically near each other. These bear on the concept of nonlocality, which is central to quantum physics and is the subject of a growing body of research.

The second feature is psychic mediumship, which Susan and I have experienced first hand. A competent medium can pick up accurate messages from deceased relatives and friends, including validating details known only to the person being read. Do such experiences prove the existence of a continuing afterlife? No, but they certainly open up the subject.

Connectedness, Cooperation, Continuity – all part of our multidimensional universe... What if any of this is true? Would it change the way you define yourself or go about your life? Would it change the way you prepare for your death? Would it change the way you think about your spiritual beliefs?

I summarized these three related ideas very quickly. They are not proven by current scientific tests. Yet there is a significant body of evidence to support each of them. I hope you see that I'm not talking about a middle way of belief that splits the difference between religion and secularism. Nor am I trying to justify what is commonly known as the supernatural. Rather, I believe we are slowly constructing a new model of the *natural* world that can validate much of both sides. On the religious side, an understanding and appreciation of the larger nonphysical world beyond our familiar physical one. On the secularist side, additional support for humanist values such as tolerance, scientific inquiry, and constructive living, beyond simply what seems to work best.

It is said that Descartes' division of the universe into matters of science and spirit opened the door to the European Enlightenment and the flowering of science. Now, I think, it is time to say that there is only one universe of science and spirit, not two. And what better institution to support this coming together than liberal religion? The traditional religionists and the secularists are stuck with rather hardened positions. A personal God or no God – this does not leave much room for exploration.

Today, I think I would have a better answer to any 13 year olds who ask me why they should buy into conventional morality. I would tell them that the universe is not a cold, meaningless collection of atoms and empty space, where everyone has to look out for him or herself, although it can seem that way in our darker moments. Rather, it is a mysterious, amazing place about which much will be discovered in their lifetimes, perhaps by them if so inclined. Finally, the evidence is rapidly growing that the universe is organized by principles we can understand and live by, principles such as connectedness, cooperation, and continuity. My best advice is to hop on board, be part of it, and join the universe. Then they'll know what to do when they find someone's wallet on the floor.

November, 2006
A New Enlightenment
Presented to the Philosophical Club of Cleveland

Readings

Akasha is a Sanskrit word meaning "ether": all-pervasive space. Originally signifying "radiation" or "brilliance" in Indian philosophy, Akasha was considered the first and most fundamental of the five elements – the others being air, fire, water, and earth. Akasha embraces the properties of all five elements; it is the womb from which everything we perceive with our senses has emerged and into which everything will ultimately re-descend. The Akashic Record is the enduring record of all that happens, and has ever happened, in space and time.

- Ervin Laszlo, "Science and the Akashic Field," 2004.

In 1909 the Harvard University psychologist William James wrote:

We live our lives like islands in the sea, or like trees in the forest. The maple and the pine may whisper to each other with their leaves, and Conanicut and Newport hear each other's foghorns. But the trees also commingle their roots in the darkness underground, and the islands also hang together through the ocean's bottom... There is a continuum of cosmic consciousness, against which our individuality builds but accidental fences, and into which our several minds plunge as into a mother-sea or reservoir.

Our "normal" consciousness is circumscribed for adaptation to our external earthly environment, but the fence is weak in spots, and fitful influences from beyond leak in, showing the otherwise unverifiable common connection. Not only psychic research, but metaphysical philosophy and speculative biology are led in their own ways to look with favor on some such "panpsychic" view of the universe as this.

Assuming this common reservoir of consciousness to exist, this bank upon which we all draw, the question is, what is its own structure? What is its inner topography? Are there subtler forms of matter which upon occasion may enter into functional connection with the individuations in the psychic sea, and then, and then only, show themselves? – so that our ordinary human experience, on its material as well as on its mental side, would appear to be only an extract from the larger psychophysical world?

- from Dean Radin, "Entangled Minds," 2006.

Enlightenment

Susan and I recently enjoyed a short and busy tour of England and Scotland, my first trip there. One of my favorite experiences was spending an hour or so in the "Enlightenment" Room at the British Museum in London. Here, collected in walls of leather-bound books in glass-enclosed display cases, are ideas and evidence assembled by British explorers, philosophers, archaeologists, and natural scientists of the late 17th and 18th centuries. This is now known as the Age of Enlightenment, a time when our collective understanding of the world went through a major change.

Virtually all the contributors were men, amateurs in the best sense of that word. Two big changes from then to now are the contributions of women and the development of professional credentials for exploration. Women double the field of explorers. The credentials requirement tends to limit it.

The Enlightenment had a strong influence on our country's founders. One strand of that influence was the departure of thinking from the dictates of established religions, particularly in natural philosophy, later called science. Another was the emergence of new political and social theory. We may marvel at that small group of American colonists piecing together a democratic republic with European societies as their only precedent. It was Enlightenment thinking that guided them. Our Founding Fathers were also amateurs in the same sense as the British explorers. They did not hire professional consultants to guide them; there weren't any.

The Enlightenment Room illustrates an important change in science (or natural philosophy). Until the early 18th century, the recognized way to learn about the world was to collect, study, and categorize specimens of interest. For example, there is a display of footwear from around the globe, collected to provide insight about anthropological variations. There is an excellent collection of natural rocks, polished to show the inner layers. Geology was still taught in the 20th century by studying such collections.

One significant 18th century change was the development of new instruments with which to observe and measure the natural world: microscopes, telescopes, precision scales, etc. King George III, of all people, strongly promoted this new way to do science, and his personal collection is in the Enlightenment Room. We may think of him as the fool who lost the colonies and ended up a crazy man, but apparently there was another side to him.

The Enlightenment was far from everybody's cup of tea in the 18th century, and it still meets resistance in many quarters of the world, including our own. Old ways of thinking have a tenacious hold on us, partly because of familiarity, partly because many authoritative establishments have been built around them, and partly because they nearly always carry a germ of truth. Yet we've had a spectacular run of about 300 years starting with Enlightenment thinking.

I believe we are in the early stages of a new Enlightenment that will change the way we understand the world – again, in a major way. Perhaps it dates back nearly 100 years to William James's prophetic remarks that I read earlier. It is growing out of a field often called consciousness studies, and is populated with scientists, philosophers, psychologists, theologians, and many other 20th century disciplines. But overall, it is still an amateur pursuit of men and women transcending the boundaries of their training. This is surely a strength, just as it was 300 years ago.

The starting point is the growing realization that human consciousness is not merely a product of our brains but a much larger phenomenon. Brains, of course, are wonderful processors of information. They sort out sensory input at incredible speeds and allow us to function in the everyday world. But there are many things brains cannot do, even with a good set of sense organs and an accurate memory bank. This is the domain of the mind, and of consciousness.

I've been following consciousness studies for over 15 years. One focus is the field of psychic phenomena – such things as telepathy, clairvoyance, precognition, and psychokinesis. We now have available careful, statistical analyses of thousands of controlled experiments in such fields, not just with humans. The analyses are detailed in a recent book by Dean Radin. He clearly shows that psychic events are real, yet still puzzling. Well bonded family members really can sense when another is in trouble. Dogs really can sense when their masters start home, even hundreds of miles away. Plants really can react to intentions of their owners. Big world events such as 9/11 really do coincide with upsets in remote random number generators. None of these things always happen. But they do happen enough to be statistically sound.

Theory. How do these connections occur? Is there a scientific explanation? The answer may be in some new theories and data emerging in the last ten years. Let's start with theory. I like the proposal of the systems theorist, Ervin Laszlo, that there is a universal information field to which we all have access, probably through what we call our subconscious. Animals and possibly inanimate things may also be connected to the same field. Laszlo calls it the A-field, in deference to the ancient idea of an Akashic field. He proposes that this concept may provide insight into many current scientific puzzles, not only in consciousness, but also in areas as wide ranging as cosmology, biology, anthropology, and quantum physics.

The proposed A-field is real, in the physical or energetic sense, but it cannot be measured scientifically, at least not yet. This information field carries the memory of everything that is, or was. It carries templates or blueprints for all organisms and things, from living organisms to planets, to galaxies and beyond.

A field of this type was known as the Akashic Record by Eastern mystics in ancient times. Somewhat related concepts are known as the quantum vacuum or the zero-point field by physicists. We are all familiar with a few fields identified in the scientific era. The gravitational field and electromagnetic fields are well known, but who has seen them or even measured them? What we measure are their effects, and that's why we easily accept them. Let's take a brief look at some of the effects that could be explained by the A-field. Some scientific puzzles.

Cosmology and the beginning of the universe. The present standard model is that our universe started with a big bang about 14 billion years ago. Measurements such as far-distant radiation and the movement of galaxies support this description. But the more we look, the more puzzling are certain aspects of the story. The biggest puzzle, perhaps, is the amazing coherence of the universe. How did the handful of physical constants evolve that have allowed 14 billion years of existence without disintegration, not to mention conditions that support life on earth and probably other planets? The probabilities of this happening are infinitesimal if the whole process occurred in a random way.

However, if our universe was born in a pre-big-bang milieu that provided guidance through informational templates from other universes, the picture changes. The big bang had references to go on. Thus we need to consider the concept of a metaverse that preceded our universe.

Biology. Biology is full of puzzles. How the parts of living organisms seem to cooperate instantly and coherently, with each other and with their environment. How the various parts develop from identical DNA into very different organs. How individual organisms cooperate with others in their species with no apparent communication. And the puzzle of evolution. Do species really mutate in response to purely random environmental effects? Or is there a pattern of development?

I'll mention one model that touches on some of these questions. It's a field theory that is consistent with the idea of the A-field. Specifically, the morphic fields that the biologist, Rupert Sheldrake, cites in discussing the development and behavior of plants and animals. He believes there is some kind of bond among similar organisms that not only provides a means of intuitive inter-communication such as within flocks of birds, but also acts as a template in the development of new members. That is, an oak tree grows from an acorn in the way other oak trees have grown by reference to a morphic or morphogenetic field of oak trees.

Human beings are not exempt from biology. There's a field theory that is much better known to many of you than Sheldrake's concept. That is the idea associated with Carl Jung that there is a collective unconscious that bonds groups of humans. The templates in this field include such things as archetypal figures.

Cultural anthropology. Let's go far afield for a moment and take note of the finding of anthropologists that human cultures seemed to develop in different parts of the planet with strikingly similar methods and objects. A lot of effort has gone into trying to find how indigenous people on different continents managed to make similar pottery or build similar pyramids. Maybe the answer is that they responded to similar information in a universal field. If birds and oak trees can do it, why not human beings?

Quantum Physics. Quantum theory was developed through some remarkable insights in response to the observation that small quantities of light sometimes act like particles and sometimes like waves. As theory and experimental confirmation progressed through the 20th century, the bedrock assumptions of classical physics began to crumble, at least at the subatomic level. Things like the reality of objects, causality, and determinism.

One of the last assumptions to go was the idea of locality. This means that one thing can influence another only in proximity to it, including signals such as radio waves. In 1964, John Bell, an Irish physicist, postulated that entities at any distance, if once connected, could still influence each other. This was experimentally confirmed for photons in 1972, and many times since then for various small particles. That is, the complementary particles are forever entangled, no matter how far from each other they travel. Locality is no longer an easy assumption. Something unaccounted for is connecting otherwise isolated objects. Entanglement.

Inevitably, some have speculated that quantum principles, and in particular, the idea of entanglement, have broader application.

One provocative idea is that everything in our universe was connected at one time, before the big bang, so everything is somehow entangled forever. Everything. An even more provocative idea I mentioned under cosmology – that the universal information field may have existed before our big bang.

Consciousness. Consciousness is being studied in many disciplines. The thorny part for most scientists is the growing evidence for psychic phenomena, or the Greek letter Psi for short.

Psi is still taboo as an acceptable academic subject. Fewer than 1% of universities worldwide have any faculty with a public interest in Psi research. Why? Simply because it is not safe, careerwise. It implies that our well-accepted model of reality is deficient. Professional skeptics ridicule any such efforts. And the history of psychic phenomena is full of fraud and nonsense. Yet... over 60% of people believe in Psi. The believers are heavily skewed to the better educated. There seems to be no correlation with religious beliefs. Statistically, the most likely Psi believer is female, under 30, well educated, creative, interested in the arts, and left-handed.

Sixty percent approval does not make it true, or an occasional psychic experience, or the ancient wisdom from sources such as the *Sutras* of Patanjali recorded over 2000 years ago. All these sources deserve respect. However, the solid support for Psi is the body of careful, controlled experiments carried out around the world over the last 75 years. These are clearly discussed in Dean Radin's book.

So, what is Psi? Any explanation has to deal with information that crosses space and time in ways that defy common sense or classical scientific models. The information interacts with objects at a distance and reaches your mind other than through your normal five senses. In ancient times, Psi was self-evident. In the age of classical science, Psi was impossible, the residue of superstition. Now what?

There have been several theories of Psi. One that was popular in the 20th century, especially in the Soviet Union, involved signals similar to electromagnetic waves. No such mechanism has been discovered. Another group might be called field theories, such as Carl Jung's collective unconsciousness or Rupert Sheldrake's morphic fields. These essentially describe rather than explain Psi effects. There are now a few approaches based on quantum theory. It is a fertile field for theorists, but most physicists still treat Psi as a hot potato while exploring the structure of the cosmos or the subatomic world.

Entanglement, only recently established as a fact in the quantum physical world, seems to be the phenomenon that can bring Psi into the scientific orbit. Entanglement does not mean that signals such as information waves pass between two minds in telepathy, for instance. It means that the two minds are already entangled because they are already part of a larger quantum system encompassing all of physical reality. This fits right in with the concept of the universal information field, the A-field. We get momentary glimpses of information about other minds, objects, the past or future, not through our senses, but because our unconscious mind is already co-existent with everything else.

Data. I've spent most of my time on a new theory to this point. Is there any hard data supporting this theory? I'm excited by an obscure article published in 1997 that finds a distinct correlation between over 2000 remote viewing trials and the time of day measured in sidereal time. Remote viewing is a disciplined psychic practice of gathering information about a distant place while in a meditative state. It was used by the US military and CIA for a variety of military objectives. Sidereal time, well known to astronomers, relates local time to the position of certain star clusters rather than to our sun, expressed in 24 hour clock time. A sidereal day is about four minutes less than a solar day.

The author, James Spottiswoode, plotted a numerical measure of the results of a series of 1400 remote viewing trials, from different laboratories over a 20 year period, versus the sidereal time of the trial. He found a well-defined peak of effectiveness at 13.5 hours sidereal. He then did the same with another series of 1000 trials and found the same peak. 13.5 hours is the time when certain star clusters are in line with the earth, but nobody would have guessed that such an alignment had anything to do with remote viewing results. Nor have I seen any explanation why one specific alignment should benefit remote viewing. This seems to be the first time that an environmental factor – in this case, galactic – was related to psychic phenomena by a scientific analysis. The internet reference is given below.

I've never had any interest in astrology. Yet, I must admit that there may be a grain of truth in the ancient notion that the orientation of celestial bodies has something to do with our lives on earth. My take on this finding is that there may be some kind of large field effect, similar to the gravitational field, which does have earthly effects. Putting 2 + 2 together, I wonder if this is a manifestation of Laszlo's universal field – the A-field. If so, we may expect further evidence to be uncovered in the coming years.

Let me summarize. I've talked about the concept of a universal information field. Such a field would shed light on many puzzling questions in fields as disparate as cosmology, biology, anthropology, quantum physics, and consciousness. The remote viewing correlation strikes me as a solid piece of data analysis that cannot be disregarded, although it will be for some time to come. The wheels of science turn very slowly.

Sometime this century, our descendants will likely be as comfortable with the universal information field as we are with the gravitational field. So, I may be jumping the gun a bit, but when Susan asks me where I am going when leaving the house, I just tell her I'm heading into the A-field.

References

Dean Radin, "Entangled Minds", 2006.
Ervin Laszlo, "Science and the Akashic Field", 2004.
S. James P. Spottiswoode, *Journal of Scientific Exploration*, Vol 11, No. 2, 1997. Also available at www.jsasoc.com/docs/JSE-LST.pdf

June, 2009
Why I Believe in Miracles

A Sermon at the First Unitarian Church of Cleveland

Reading 1

In May, 1962, Vittorio Michelli, a middle-aged Italian man, was admitted to the Military Hospital of Verona, Italy, suffering from a large, painful mass on his left side that severely limited the range of motion of the hip. X-rays revealed extensive destruction of the bones of the pelvis and hip joint. A biopsy showed a substantial carcinoma. Neither surgery nor radiation was prescribed. He was immobilized in a plaster cast and was sent to the Military Hospital at Trente. He spent the next ten months there without any treatment despite ongoing destruction of bone from the tumor, as well as progressive loss of all active movement of the left lower limb and progressive physical deterioration. By this time, Michelli was literally falling apart – the mass continuing to enlarge, eating away the bone and supporting structures that kept his left leg attached to the rest of his body. He was emaciated and unable to eat.

A year after the original diagnosis, in May, 1963, he was taken by friends to Lourdes. It must have been a difficult journey. On arrival his friends bathed him in the holy waters. Following the bath, he reported sensations of heat moving through his body, as well as an immediate return of his appetite and a resurgence of energy.

Then his friends lugged him back to the hospital in Trente, still in plaster, where he began to gain weight and become more active. A month later, the doctors consented to remove his cast. An

X-ray found that the tumor was smaller than before. It continued to diminish and finally disappeared. Continued X-rays tracked an astonishing event. The destroyed bone began to regrow and completely reconstructed itself. Two months after Lourdes, he went for a walk. Here is an excerpt from a later medical report:

"A remarkable reconstruction of the iliac bone and cavity has taken place. The X-rays from 1963 to 1969 confirm without doubt that an overwhelming bone reconstruction has taken place of a type unknown in the annals of world medicine. We ourselves, during a university and hospital career of over 45 years spent largely in the study of tumors and neoplasms of all kinds of bone structures and having ourselves treated hundreds of such cases, have never encountered a single spontaneous bone reconstruction of such a nature... A medical explanation of the cure was sought and none could be found. He did not undergo specific treatment. A completely destroyed articulation was completely reconstructed without any surgical intervention. The lower limb which was useless became sound, the prognosis is indisputable, and the patient is alive and in a flourishing state of health nine years after his return from Lourdes."

Reading 2

An unanswered question in science, which occurs to every wide-eyed child, is: Why does anything exist? Why is there something rather than nothing? Scientists come closest to these queries when they ask what existed before the big bang, the primordial explosion that signaled the beginning of the universe. The answer generally given is, nothing. By any stretch of the imagination, this is the greatest miracle ever conceived. If scientists are willing to believe that something as stupendous as the entire universe came from nothing, it's difficult to imagine what they would not believe. If skeptics can swallow the tenets of modern cosmology about the origins of the universe, why should they go ballistic when a simple cancer up and disappears when splashed with a little holy water?

Both readings are taken from an article in Science and Spirit, May 2003, by Larry Dossey, MD, entitled "The Measure of Miracles."

Sermon

The grotto and spring at Lourdes, in Southwestern France, has been the site of thousands of alleged healings in the 150 years since

14 year old Bernadette first saw a vision of Mary. It draws 4 to 6 million visitors a year. The Roman Catholic Church and an independent medical commission continue to investigate the occurrences. To date, they have certified 67 healings as bona fide, that is, real and not explainable by current medical or psychological knowledge. The miraculous healing I described in my first reading was one of those 67, accepted by the Church in 1976, 13 years after it occurred.

Is anyone here uncomfortable with that story? Is it (a) because it cannot be true, as described, or (b) because there is no such thing as a God that intervenes in human affairs? Or holy water. Or perhaps you agree with me that it is probably true but not yet explainable by today's scientific knowledge.

There happens to be a small minority opinion about the Lourdes healings that focuses on the molecular structure of the spring water. It is plausible but by no means proven. I could have made the question even harder by recounting one of the documented healings that have no connection to Lourdes or holy water, but simply to traditional prayer, or even more elusive, to a nighttime vision without prayer.

For today's purpose, let me define miracles as events or observations of some significance that have no conceivable scientific explanation. They are a subset of anomalies, that is, observations, events, or facts that are well outside normal expectations or existing understandings. More about anomalies in a moment.

In common usage, many things are called miracles that are simply unusual events that may have a reasonable scientific or statistical explanation unknown to the participants. Or they are normal coincidences. For example, a best-selling book in 1997 called "Small Miracles" is full of coincidences and pleasant outcomes. To most of us who are not medical professionals, the birth of a child is easy to call a miracle, as is the remission of a cancer through strenuous application of modern medicine.

Here are two recurring observations outside the realm of medical cures that I consider miraculous, although you may not consider them significant.

Many identical twins immediately sense a traumatic event experienced by the other twin, whatever the distance between them.

This is not the same as the many documented cases where twins separated at birth show many of the same life choices and habits years later. Most such instances are reasonably explained by genetics. My focus is on the instant communication of feelings, even pain, between the twins, most evident at times of death or physical injury of one. In one study, about 30% of identical twins reported this phenomenon.

How about pet owners? Some of my favorite examples of unusual communication, as reported by the biologist Rupert Sheldrake, are documented cases of pet dogs that appear to know when their masters *decide* to come home, even hundreds of miles away – at which time the dogs get up and station themselves at the door or window. These dogs generally have a long bonded relationship with their masters. These studies have carefully filtered out the usual explanations for pets going to the door: regular time of day, sound of car approaching, etc.

These examples are drawn from a very large body of unusual occurrences, many very well documented. Time is short, so let's stick to medical cures, twins, and sensitive dogs. What do we make of these? Most thoughtful people respond in one of two ways, depending on whether their orientation to the world is through traditional religion or secular humanism.

Religious people tend to see the intervention of God in human affairs, at least in cases of healing. I've expressed my view of intervention in another sermon when I talked about the phenomenon of angels. I believe we can and do occasionally receive communications from higher levels of consciousness, yet I don't believe we can specify when or about what. I described this process as similar to our internal organs getting some direction from our brain, but functioning most of the time without any external instructions. I don't think this makes me a theist. Maybe a consciousnessist. I have not studied Karl Jung, but I believe my speculation is consistent with his ideas about the collective unconscious.

The secular population, whether educated scientifically or not, often sees psychological issues around a belief in miracles. They talk about delusion and fraud, and are proud to be called skeptics. The more open-minded secularists admit there may be a scientific explanation for these unusual events that has not yet surfaced. In any case, they find little interest in the subject.

Although I counted myself among the secularists for many years, I'm drawn to a third approach. That is, I'm interested in miracles and unexplainable events, large and small, because they are clues to future understanding about the nature of our universe. My interest is also influenced by my work life, about which I'll give an example shortly in a brief side trip through anomalies.

Anomalies are observations, events, or facts that are well outside normal expectations or existing models. They often arise from mistakes or accidents, such as a new material made in a laboratory when the experiment goes awry, a data point that doesn't fit a correlation, even a kitchen concoction that turned out far better, or worse, than the last time it was made. Some common anomalies can be, and are, resolved quickly. Others take longer. Some even take centuries.

Some of the biggest steps in scientific history resulted from recognition of an anomaly in familiar observations. Copernicus saw that the orbits of planets were not consistent with an earth-centered universe. For about a hundred years, physicists knew about the anomaly posed by light, namely the observation that photons can behave like particles or waves, depending on the experiment conducted. In the early 20th century, Max Planck and other physicists tackled that anomaly in developing quantum physics.

Anomalies are not uncommon in research laboratories. They often lead to substantial progress. I worked in chemical technology for 30 years. Recently I listed the 10 major accomplishments of my work life and the primary reasons for success. I found that 3 out of 10 were due to attention to anomalies. One of those was a project to develop a better product. A series of samples were made and tested, and one stood out as markedly superior. It was retested: superior again. When we tried to prepare it again by our standard procedure, it was no better than the others. This was very frustrating for all concerned. After checking all the preparation notebooks, we finally discovered that a technician had left that sample overnight without its final heat treatment because he left early for a doctor's appointment. New samples were prepared incorporating the overnight step, and all were superior. Whatever changes happened overnight were very subtle. The superior samples could not be distinguished from the others with available instrumentation. They don't give Nobel prizes for this sort of thing, or even a bonus, but the new product added millions of dollars to the company's sales.

Chemical technology is sprinkled with laboratory anomalies from mistakes or accidents that led to superior new products. Vulcanized rubber, Bakelite, Saran wrap, Scotchgard, and Teflon come to mind. In all these cases, scientific understanding was developed after the event. What started as a few anomalies morphed into the field of polymer chemistry.

Apparent anomalies in scientific work share certain characteristics. First of all, most of them are not true anomalies, i.e. not real. They are mostly flawed observations or data caused by human errors, wishful thinking, faulty instruments, inaccurate memory, ignorance of the underlying science, or just plain fraud. These probably total well over 90%. Skeptics provide a valuable service by calling attention to such flaws, as it is very easy to get excited about apparent anomalies. So, the first task is to check and then recheck the data again. Discard the 90%+ that aren't real and move on.

Many people take a wrong turn at this point, and it's a critical one. They also dismiss data because the data don't fit existing models, the collective prior understanding of the nature of things. They lose the potential value of having an anomaly presented to them on a silver platter. If you are pursuing commercial objectives, the anomaly could be worth a lot of money.

Permit me a brief aside. During my 20th century working years, I became convinced that the American technical culture supported the pursuit of anomalous results more easily than did older cultures such as European and Japanese. I understood the reason to be the different roles of authority. In the older cultures, the opinions of the chief scientist were often treated as law, to be disregarded at great personal peril. The differences are probably less at present because of the rapid spread of American-style education and work attitudes.

Back to anomalies. The quality of data, or evidence, is just as important outside the laboratory, and the same rules apply. As far as I know, the Roman Catholic authorities and independent medical advisors treat reports of medical miracles with utmost skepticism. Very few instances make it through the process and are deemed miracles. For instance, if the patient was taking medication at the time of an alleged miracle cure, a miracle was generally ruled out.

Communication of feelings between identical twins is well known to those involved but not something the rest of us can relate to easily. Similar communication of dramatic events, but less remarkable, is reported for other siblings, mothers and children, and long-time partners. The strength or frequency of communication is roughly in line with the degree of bonding, genetic or otherwise. I know of two married couples who sometimes know what the other is dreaming. That may be part of the same process. However, nobody knows how it occurs. Of course, that's a poor reason to dismiss it.

I'm not a dog owner, but I am fascinated by the finding that many pets can sense when their master decides to come home. I've seen videos of dogs in empty houses get up and station themselves at the door or front window just when their masters make that decision, even hundreds of miles away. I would love to be around when we figure that one out.

Everyday anomalies, scientific oddities, and miraculous events are very different, of course, but our way of thinking about them should follow the same logic. Are they real? If so, do they have an explanation in existing knowledge? If so, they are no longer anomalies. If not, don't dismiss them. Both history and personal experience suggest that we accept the facts and incorporate them in our future thinking and scientific theorizing. That is where hard-line skeptics often refuse to go. Perhaps their dislike of the religious overtones rather than discomfort with science stops them. A third possibility is a misunderstanding of science itself.

Sometimes I hear, "show me the double-blind studies" from skeptics. Such studies are an elegant statistical procedure in clinical studies, common in the testing of new medicines but certainly not applicable to one-of-a-kind miracles. You often have to deal with the facts as they are available. I also hear, "what scientific laws are involved here." In truth, there are no laws out on the frontier of scientific understanding. They come later. Copernicus, for example, created new laws to explain puzzling facts. Rarely do the laws come first, and only to a master of mental experiments like Einstein. In short, I consider science to be an attitude toward the physical world, not just a way to explain things with accepted methods. In a similar way, I also consider Unitarian-Universalism to be an attitude toward the spiritual world that is free of the rules and dogma of the past.

My guess is that a new scientific discipline that will account for today's anomalies and miracles will be well advanced in the next few years. It will include new ways to characterize the physics and biology of consciousness, and most exciting, it will be based on reproducible experimental data. Today we have available several interesting speculations about such things as universal information fields and multiple universes that are closer to science fiction than to proven laws. Tomorrow we will pin them down. That's the history of science on earth, and I see no reason that it will change. It will just happen faster.

Susan and I attended a conference about science and consciousness earlier this month. I was quite surprised to learn that progress in understanding miraculous events such as I summarized is moving much faster than I had imagined a month ago. The basis is a new extension of quantum physics principles such as nonlocality and entanglement from the subatomic realm to the macro world – that is, the familiar world we inhabit. The accelerating speed of science is breathtaking.

One more aside – an opinion I've offered in other presentations. Our understanding of both the physical and nonphysical world, including many questions traditionally associated with religion, is changing rapidly. The core of this renaissance seems to be a mixture of quantum physics, modern cosmology, biology, and probes of the nature of consciousness. It is very important that modern religion, including Unitarian-Universalism, take notice of this movement. Otherwise, young people with the same old religious questions as the rest of us will not find spiritual satisfaction within our walls. We are often defined as a home for 20th century humanism. As important as humanism is, as a guide to living in the here and now, it is not the future of religion and spiritual growth.

Conclusion

A scientific anomaly in one age is usually incorporated in our expanding knowledge base a generation or so later. Max Planck was reported to say that a new scientific truth does not triumph by convincing its opponents to see the light, but rather because its opponents eventually die.

Earlier I asked what we can make of these strange anomalies, some of which are called miracles. My answer is to not dismiss them because they don't fit our current understanding of the world, nor because they are often co-opted by traditional religious organizations. Instead, treat them as a factual and experiential basis for tomorrow's knowledge, yet to be worked out. The prospect is exciting and life enriching.

IDEAS and REFLECTION

April, 1999
Our Cars, Our Selves

It's said that American men organize their personal histories by the cars they drove. As... I moved to California while I still had the '72 Dart. Or... I met my wife just after I got the '63 Mustang. Or... my Dad taught me to drive in the '47 Plymouth with the un-synchronized clutch. (The last one is mine.)

Our lives and our cars are very closely matched. I don't want to upset anyone, but I would venture that most men remember all the cars they owned, in which order, more easily than the relationships they were in, and certainly in which order. You might say that cars leave an indelible memory that other attachments often lack.

Of course I'm exaggerating, but not much. You may have noticed that many women, intelligent and accomplished, worldly and wise, simply treat their cars as something to get them from one place to another. Very few men think this way, and if they say they do, they're probably lying out of some notion of correctness.

Why is this? Are we men so obtuse or insensitive or immature that we confuse life matters of greater importance with those of little or no importance? I don't think so. Cars, by themselves, are obviously low on a scale compared, say, with serious illness or the inflation rate. However, as symbols, they represent values of considerable significance to being a man in the twentieth century. Values such as ownership, independence, and respect.

Until we own our first house, the car is our primary possession. Even home owning is a vague, uneasy concept when the bank owns over ninety percent of it.

From about age fifteen, the overriding goal of young men is independence from family and direction from above. A car provides that sense, flawed as it may be. It assumes even greater importance when we find that we never really get away from direction from above.

And respect. Cars are a statement of how we wish to be seen in the world. This does not necessarily mean the biggest and most powerful car, as few of us see ourselves as powerful. There are many other important statements one can make with the selection of a car. I am sophisticated. I am sexy. I am different. I disdain American goods. I believe in American goods. I am wealthy. I am discriminating about quality. I am a little bit wild and crazy. I am tough. And so on.

I'll tell you about my first Volkswagen and, if you wish, you can decide what statements I was making. That's OK; I don't mind. After all, I made the statements for someone to notice.

But first, a brief note about that remark about learning to drive. A few years ago I participated in a retreat with mostly middle aged men. The topic was "Our Fathers, Our Selves". We talked all weekend about our relationships with our fathers and there were more than a few tears shed in this group of well-educated professional men. The single most emotional topic was whether or not your father taught you to drive. If he was dead or away at war, it was OK that someone else taught you. But if he was available, and turned the job over to someone else, it seemed to leave a scar for life. For many of the participants, this was the most important way for a father to show his love for his son.

Yes, I know there are far more serious issues between parents and children. But... are you still thinking that the symbolic meaning of cars is over-rated?

Now for the Volkswagen. Incidentally, it's important to pronounce that the German way, FolksVagen. Not to a Dodge owner, of course.

My first new car was a '55 VW Beetle, with the small rear window, mechanical or flipper turn signals, and no gas gauge. VW introduced them in the US the year before. I was charter member 531 of the VW Club of America, which allowed me to attach a tag to my license plate and receive periodic tips to modify and enjoy the car, along with upbeat testimonials. What a statement this car made! I won't bore you with all the adventures the VW and I got into, but just a few notes for flavor.

* In the early days, when you came upon another VW on the road, you pulled over and compared gas mileage.

* It came with a hand crank, which was often necessary to start the car in the cold New England winter.

* My buddies once lifted it up and set it down between a stop sign and a fireplug.

* Driving cross country, we normally kept the accelerator pushed to the floor, resulting in speeds of 70 mph on flat land, considerably more or less on hills.

* We used to triple date in the VW. That's hard to imagine now.

I had three more VW cars over the next 25 years, but I will never forget that first one. It was dark blue. It was mine.

June, 1999
Equilibrium

I've found that people who have had intensive training or experience in one discipline tend to think that way about other things, even in dreams. Athletes frame issues in terms of competition, stamina, physical skills. Musicians often see the world as harmonic changes, melodies, ensemble playing. Artists deal with color and texture. Accountants have balance sheets. Historians focus on trends and cycles.

I had some intense years of education and 30 years of practice in chemical engineering. It can be annoying at times, but it is not surprising that my dreams and my wakeful musings often take the form of physical chemical phenomena. I'll give some examples of one concept that keeps returning for me.

Dynamic equilibrium refers to an overall state of equilibrium where the individual components (molecules, for example) are quite busy moving about, following their own inclinations. A covered glass of water looks quite at rest, but at the air/water interface huge numbers of water molecules are becoming gaseous water vapor every second, and an equal number are condensing to liquid. There is a known fraction of water vapor in the air space that changes with temperature. A different liquid at the same temperature would have a different fraction of vaporized molecules in the air. Change the temperature or change the liquid, and a new equilibrium occurs. But if you break the glass, the rules change.

You're probably way ahead of me in finding social or political analogs for the glass of water at equilibrium. Armies facing each other in trenches. The fortunes of a company. The relative status of majority and minority groups in a society. The standing of a professional sports team. The amount of carbon dioxide or ozone in the air. Marriages.

In these examples, equilibrium can and does prevail for relatively long times, even decades or more, despite individual efforts to cause change – despite the individual units going their own way. Sometimes there is a gradual "temperature" change that allows new equilibrium positions to be set in place, while the system remains intact. Sometimes the glass is broken.

Trench warfare ended fairly quickly as tanks, and then airplanes, were introduced. Companies can be raised or ruined by changes of leadership, but the real glass-breakers are usually inventions. Social changes, for good or evil, are often dependent on the emergence of special leaders, as sports teams are highly dependent on superstars. Our atmosphere is changing more this century because of the burning of fossil fuels than in all of recorded history. Still, it feels in equilibrium at the level of our human time scale.

All marriages evolve. The state of marital equilibrium in our society continually shifts in response to numerous factors, and is totally disrupted by others. What is fascinating to those who study marriages is that the same factor may shift equilibrium in one marriage and break up another. Things like job changes, moves, health crises, or the fortunes of relatives.

Right now there are some very significant shifts in the equilibrium of large systems going on about us, including some major glass breaking. In times of peace I don't think we've ever experienced anything as disruptive to the way things were as the digital computer. Whole industries such as retail and publishing are in upheaval, just to name two areas. The airplane seemed huge, but the computer is even bigger. Space exploration and the inevitable discovery of extraterrestrial beings will break some very big glasses. Rapidly accumulating knowledge of physiology and health is certainly changing the way we will live in the near future.

Speaking of the way we live, I sense a deteriorating equilibrium between the haves and have-nots in the world and in our country that will either have to be adjusted within the system, or will shift as a result of a major system upheaval. The current disparity in distribution of resources, coupled with the widespread availability of new technology, resembles the bottle of water that has been carefully placed in a very cold freezer. Once the ice starts to form, the process moves quickly. The resulting system is composed of ice crystals and broken glass.

How soon will it change, and how rapidly? My guess is that new leaders will emerge around the world who will force the shift to a new, more equitable equilibrium. I see a third party in the United States gaining national power on the platform of equity, probably within ten years or so. But this is a question about the rate of change, and chemical engineers have many ways to describe such things. So do accountants and musicians and athletes and historians.

Dealing with large social issues as well as small ones should not be restricted to experts in any one field. We all can contribute, whatever discipline shapes our dreams.

May, 2000

The Right Thing

In April, I was privileged to attend a tribute to Charles Vanik at the Jewish Community Center in Beachwood. It commemorated the 25th anniversary of the Jackson-Vanik amendment to the Trade Act of 1974. The amendment required a country to meet specific free-emigration criteria in order to have certain economic benefits in trade with the United States. This legislation was a primary instrument in allowing over two million people to emigrate from the Soviet Union in the subsequent 25 years to the U.S., Israel, and other countries – Jews and other minorities. Just since 1989, over 6000 have settled in the Cleveland area.

Vanik, from a Catholic Czech heritage, represented the East Side of Cleveland in the U.S. House from 1954 to 1981 after 20 years of public life as a lawyer and politician in Cleveland. He co-sponsored the amendment with Senator "Scoop" Jackson of Washington State. Eighty-seven years old, retired in Florida, he and his wife came to town to attend the tribute. The gathering included hundreds of business, professional, religious, and local political leaders, a current U.S. Senator and Representatives, and a large contingent from the local Russian-Jewish community.

Among the many outstanding speeches were two from older immigrants in heavily accented but heartfelt words, and one from a young woman in graduate school who immigrated at three years old – without accent. Lev Polyakin, the Assistant Concert Master of the Cleveland Orchestra and one of the immigrants, played two selections beautifully.

The emotional peak of the celebration was provided by a group of older immigrants called the Mazel Tov Senior Chorus. They sang *Hava Nagillah* in Hebrew, *Moscow Nights* in Russian, and ended with *God Bless America*. The hundreds of guests all stood and joined in the last one. I doubt there were many dry eyes in the auditorium at that point, but I was unable to see clearly. Yes, it was sentimental. It was also a moment of considerable pride in this nation.

Patriotism is not easy to come by in these freewheeling times. When I was a reserve officer in our peacetime Army, I was willing to serve as needed, based on trust in our national leadership. Yet, the strength of my patriotism was never really tested. I reached normal retirement from the active reserve in 1965; my unit was activated for Viet Nam one year later. So my patriotism still carries a small rosy aura from my memories of World War II as a child, and from my early education in American history.

Periodically we read alarming statistics showing how little most young people know about our history and current political questions. It seems to be less in each successive generation. But consider that the adult world appears to be largely geared toward acquisition. Why should we expect the young to disregard that teaching in their own lives?

My guess is that patriotism is way down the list for young people and they will, in turn, pass their priorities to the next generation. Since I am 50 years older than a teenager, the gap in values looks huge to me, but it is made of many incremental changes from year to year, decade to decade. Each one looked small and was often associated with good intentions. But the sum is large.

Some of the changes that have distanced people from their nation and their governance include the abolition of universal military service, minimal requirements for citizenship (remember Civics classes?) and the excesses of the free press in reporting the personal failings of leaders. The list might also include the gradual reforming of high school pre-college curricula into preparation for SAT exams, at the expense of cultural education, and to use a very old phrase, moral development. These and other changes were not forced on an unwilling public.

There is another big change in these 50 years that impacts community life, namely the ascendance of single-purpose goal setting at the expense of balance. This model, widely taught by "success" motivators and management consultants, has overtaken our corporate community – the focus on the bottom line and the stock price. Within my memory, considerably more attention was paid to serving all one's constituencies in business: customers, suppliers, employees, community, and government. The prevailing message is all too clear: Do not dilute your efforts in pursuing financial security by such distractions as citizenship, cultural education, the arts, spiritual development, and perhaps even family. It's not surprising that citizenship and its partner, patriotism, get so little attention.

We all, young and old alike, are in this ongoing experiment in democracy. Likewise, we all need to be reminded periodically of our good fortune to live in a country that sometimes, amidst the contentious and self-serving posturing that often passes for news, uses its enormous power in the world to do the right thing. Thank you, Charlie Vanik, and thanks to those who realized the anniversary deserved a celebration.

In May, I attended a memorial service for my uncle at a national veteran's cemetery in Milwaukee. Uncle Tom had been a Navy pilot in World War II. He was our family hero. Some of the older men who showed up had their VFW caps on. At the conclusion of the orations, *Taps* was played. I joined them in saluting the flag.

God Bless America, land that I love;
Stand beside her, and guide her,
Through the night with the light from above.
From the mountains, to the prairies,
To the ocean, white with foam,
God Bless America, my home sweet home;
God Bless America, my home sweet home.

Irving Berlin, 1918

June, 2000
Teenagers, 2000

This is a simple story about people, mostly in their mid teens, and a kitten.

John, about 16 years old, lives part of the time next door with his father, members of one of the numerous splintered families that are spread across our modern suburban scene. His mother lives somewhere nearby, and a much older half brother stays here from time to time with a wife and a small child.

We've had no conflict with this household in eleven years of being neighbors, but little contact. There have been concerns about huge bonfires in the backyard on many occasions, outbursts of firecrackers, and late night gatherings. Still, live and let live has been the controlling mode. A couple of times, John did some garden work for us and was a conscientious worker. We couldn't count on his availability; for long periods he must have lived with his mother.

This spring, the house – the front steps to be specific – has become an after-school hangout for teenagers. Since I work at home, I've observed this almost daily. My wife Susan works long hours, and only sees them now and then in the early evening. Since we are a substantial distance from any high school or public transportation, the hangout clearly has taken shape as the teens have obtained driving licenses and access to cars, both junkers and late-model family cars.

The group, both boys and girls, seems to consist mainly of outsiders, those who do not have scheduled team practice, music lessons, or other sanctioned behaviors to attend. Most of them smoke cigarettes, have multiple tattoos and weird haircuts, spit a lot, and use extremely foul language. Many of the boys have shaved heads and some have shirts or jackets with "skinhead" printed on them. A large German Imperial flag sometimes is displayed in the front yard during hangout hours. The flag has an iron cross on it, but not Nazi symbols. I don't know whether alcohol or drugs are part of the social mix.

The background music, played loudly, is mostly rock. Yet one day recently I heard a classical music station for the better part of an hour. Perhaps there's one real outsider in the group who wanted equal time.

So it's not surprising that there has been some reaction on the street, although we are not a typical suburban neighborhood – mostly small homes with the town water treatment plant at the end of the street, next to the hangout. A young couple has called the police a few times because of the noise and cars, perhaps also with concern about the flag. There have been a few casual conversations about "the problem" as the weather has turned warmer and summer approaches.

I set up a small studio above our garage last winter, close to the hangout, where I spend a few hours a week working on stained glass. One afternoon, on an impulse, I went over to the hangout, where one boy and three girls were sitting on the steps, waiting for John to arrive. I'm sure that they saw me as a complaint walking in. Instead, I asked if any of them were interested in art. There were some cautious affirmatives, but what did I want? I explained that I was doing a stained glass project and they might be interested in seeing it in progress. So they agreed and followed me up to the studio. One of the girls, bedecked in leather and studs and lots of body jewelry, was carrying a kitten with a similar ornamented collar.

We spent about 20 minutes there, where I showed them my tools and designs and a partially done piece. I found out some of their interests. The boy liked photography and was starting college next year. One girl was thinking about architecture, although she had a year of high school left. One girl had yet to complete a summer session to finish high school; she liked to draw. What, I asked. Well, mainly tattoos. She seemed to know the most about art materials and colors.

Impulse number two hit me. I asked if any of them wanted to earn some money doing yard work. We had a very large pile of bark mulch to be spread under shrubs and in flower gardens, along with some weeding, and had difficulty finding anyone to do it. This raised some interest, as the group had been worrying about finding some money to pay for shots for the kitten. So, we set a time two days later when Susan, the family gardener, would take some time off work and meet with a crew to get the work done. I figured three or four at most would show up. In the discussion I also found that some of them had late afternoon and evening jobs, probably at fast food restaurants or pizza parlors.

At the appointed time two days later, eight teenagers (including John) showed up and accomplished a lot of work in two hours, spreading the entire pile of mulch and more. They made enough to pay for the shots and have two hours apiece at minimum wage. It was a sight to see, all these jeweled and tattooed bodies digging, raking, carting, and hauling. Enough neighbors saw it that the "problem" became much less a concern. I wouldn't be surprised if this exercise also elevated the group's collective self esteem a couple of notches. When they were finished they cleaned up nicely.

One more note, a small item. Susan has always provided cold drinks for people working outside our house on hot days like this one. So she prepared the usual trays of home-made iced tea for the crew. Although welcome, she was told three or four times that "you don't have to be nice to us" by different members.

I understand the suspicion. Yet, the work was needed and they needed to earn a few dollars. A classic *quid pro quo* situation. In time, I'm confident, they will understand that Susan was doing what came naturally. Some of them may even incorporate it in their emerging value systems, alongside care for a friend's kitten.

October, 2000
Veterans Day

*Published in the Cleveland Plain Dealer as an Op-Ed Column titled
"Peace: the highest honor for veterans"*

My birthday is November 11. When I was small there was always a parade and the older kids stayed home from school – because it was my birthday. Whatever the day of the week, I had a party with a whipped cream cake from a German bakery. I felt quite special.

By the time I entered elementary school I understood the reason for parades. Soon the cakes disappeared too. I don't know whether that was the result of wartime butter and sugar rationing or the overnight de-Germanization of our society, but it was an unfortunate loss.

Much greater losses became evident as the war continued. The lists of wounded and missing; the increasing number of gold stars in front windows signifying the death of a son or husband.

Since that time I've found my birthday to be a sober day, not just because it is often grey with the imminent threat of snow. I read the newspaper stories about veterans and think about the families I know that were forever changed by war. Stories about people who never knew their fathers, whose lives ended in a military cemetery before their 25th birthday. Stories about groups of veterans returning to Normandy or Iwo Jima or Saigon, to see how it had changed or not changed and to consider why they had survived and why their friends had not.

For wars are about survival – personal, small groups, peoples and nations. Armies have always run on the fuel of personal survival. On the larger scale, it is what they are fighting about, if the war is legitimate.

Legitimate? Well, yes, if they arise from legitimate conflicts between armed groups or nations after statesmanship has failed. Unfortunately, the core conflicts are too easily obscured, and then overwhelmed, by the baser motivations of ambition, pride, anger, greed, and revenge.

It is often said that World War II was legitimate in that the survival of democratic values was at stake – not just among the Allied countries but also within the Axis countries. History tells us that the conflict was born on the original day my birthday commemorates, in the form of a punitive peace. For the next 20 years, statesmanship was inadequate in addressing legitimate survival issues, allowing some of the lowest motives in human history to grow like weeds in a vacant lot.

Has diplomacy improved since those dismal years between the world wars? Some, certainly. The rebuilding of the Axis countries as well as the Allies may be the best example. The post-World War II initiatives by the United States, largely bipartisan, were developed around survival of the peoples and nations involved. It is hard to imagine the state of the world now had they been left to struggle alone.

U.S. policy through the Cold War, in Southeast Asia, and elsewhere in the world can be viewed through the same lens, and it is not hard to conclude that legitimate survival issues were sometimes considered secondary to other issues, some less than honorable.

Our country has been a great power for less than a human lifetime, perhaps too short to learn how to behave like one. But it must be required of powerful nations to look beyond ambition and revenge, and to focus on legitimate issues. Sometimes this means being active peace keepers – a role that would not have been debated in the recent (2000) presidential campaign if the candidates had shown more sense of history.

Today, the conflicts in the Middle East are essentially about survival, but as usual, also about pride, ambition, anger, revenge, and a tangle of political and religious issues. Yet, survival of both Israel and the Palestinians is something that can and should be addressed by those nations that have learned from history. How long can people be born, live and die in a place called the West Bank?

A clear statement of this understanding by the United States and other major world powers could be a step toward resolution. It would also be an appropriate way to honor the veterans of past wars – by showing that we have learned something from their struggles.

There's no mail delivery on November 11, so I usually get my birthday cards early. Cheerful, silly cards about not having enough candles or getting stuck at 49. So, each year on the 11th I set the newspaper down and reread the cards and try to put things together. Celebrations and sadness. Thoughts on survival.

It's still a special kind of birthday.

October, 2003

The Anger Virus

Dear Kids:

I have an uncontrollable age-related urge to collect my thoughts on how to have a good life. Since writing is the best way for me, this is more or less a brief essay. Brief, because it's not difficult to explain, just difficult to do.

The main obstacle between us and a good life is anger. A close second, perhaps, is irrational fear, which is often tangled up with anger. Rational fear from imminent violence or life-threatening disease, for example, is obviously debilitating, but not persistent. Although I'll stick to anger in these notes, there are many parallels with irrational fear. The way to deal with anger is to recognize it, understand it, and minimize it. That's about it. The rest of the essay is exposition, as we say in playwriting.

So what's a good life? One in which you have frequent opportunity to experience joy. One where you continually develop your understanding of self, the human condition, and your connection to the universe – all, of course, limited by your knowledge and experience. One where your behavior and accomplishments are consistent with your understandings.

Broad knowledge and experience make all this harder, because they open up so many opportunities to make both good and bad choices. Take a good look at some mentally handicapped people.

Their options are very limited, but their ability to experience joy is often overwhelming to the rest of us.

Needless to say, joy and understanding rarely come from material accumulation, entertainment, the adulation of others, or even worldly accomplishments. These compare poorly with noticing the first crocuses in spring, forming a new insight while reading a book, or watching a child learn to walk. But you already know that.

Back to anger. It's true that anger, when controlled and channeled, can energize constructive achievement. However, it's also true that anger underlies most, if not all, destructive achievement, from vandalism to war to genocide. I can count very few examples of constructive anger, but countless cases of destructive anger.

But what about anger at blatant injustice, greed, or arrogance? Real achievers take note of these evils and set about challenging them. The rest of us too often just stay angry, unable to take useful action. Sometimes the successful action is not a confrontation but an end run along a new, creative path. An example is the civil rights movement. Success came from thoughtful combinations of end runs and carefully chosen confrontations, not from angry retaliation. A principal reason for that was the spiritual basis of the movement. Incidentally, the practical lesson here is to pick your own battlefields rather than let your enemy pick them. All the great military leaders knew that by heart.

Anger, like irrational fear, is stuck in the past. It has roots in all those bad things that happened to us, often long ago and usually forgotten by everyone except ourselves. Miserable childhoods, abusive relationships, uncaring parents, flawed marriages, humiliations, unfair criticism, and raw deals of all varieties. All real stuff. I continue to see many people carrying these things around like permanent backpacks just waiting to be reopened so they can all spill out yet again. Far too often the contents get spilled onto children, and the old events infect a new generation. We become carriers of the anger virus (anger.exe?), infecting those who are close to us. This virus is especially adept at wiping out opportunities for joy.

The virus is widespread among middle-aged divorced folks, both men and women. I came upon it frequently in my single years, though it took a while to recognize it. I once attended a weekend introductory workshop at the Gestalt Institute where at least half the participants were, themselves, counselors and psychotherapists. We sat around the floor on pillows, and I noticed that several people brought their own pillows. At one point we were invited to beat the pillows or stomp on them to let it all come out. I was surprised that many of the pillows represented ex's. It seems to me that it would be more useful to stomp on one's anger at the ex than on the ex. The ex has enough problems coping with the same marriage.

Anger is largely learned, although a propensity for anger may be genetic. Although I haven't seen any research on the subject, I wouldn't be surprised to learn that a developing fetus can pick up the anger virus. I believe that fetuses can pick up whether the mother is disappointed in its gender, which is a strong argument for the parents not knowing gender until birth. This would be a case of pre-birth learning, not genetics.

Children do exhibit varying degrees of irritability when very young, usually ascribed to physical causes like digestive problems. That's not the same as anger. However, anger can grow from simple irritability if it is reinforced in any number of ways, as "He has his grandfather's bad disposition." Imagine carrying that one around your whole life.

It is commonplace that males are angrier than females. Anger often accompanies our win/lose orientation to life, fueled by that great mixed blessing known as testosterone. These observations are pretty sound, but it strikes me that most of it is learned behavior. Two pieces of evidence support this view. One is the existence of cultures here and there through history where men and women are about equal in such traits. The other is the current scene where many young women who go through education and career choices similar to their male counterparts turn out to be oriented much the same, including anger. All in all, I vote for learning, not genes.

Not everybody is angry. Lots of people including some well known world-class achievers experienced terrible childhoods. Many have survived their beginnings and young adult years without being crippled by anger and fear. A common occurrence was that one person, somewhere along the line, took interest in the young person and made the difference. That's often a relative, teacher, a supervisor, or social worker. We seem to be programmed to strive for a good life not crippled by anger. The key is a readiness to trust someone. Too much early anger training can make that step very hard.

One of the diseases promoted by the anger virus is called victimology. There are entire organizations dedicated to keeping that disease alive and well. Caroline Myss, author of "Anatomy of the Spirit", challenges her audiences very strongly to leave that behind and get on with life. She tells the story how she was invited to Scotland to give a workshop. One of the attendees was very anxious to have a few private minutes with Myss. The first thing she said was not her name or life interest or a spiritual question, but "I'm a survivor of childhood abuse." And that was how she saw herself. Unfortunately, she was consumed by the virus.

Another group of people for whom the virus is deeply embedded are some surviving families of real victims. Life is very unkind to those who lose a loved one, especially a child, to violence. The virus shows up in news accounts about parole hearings for the perpetrators of the violence, where the remaining family asks the judge to keep the prisoner locked up indefinitely. Even after 20 or 30 years. They say, "30 years does not compensate for my child's life." Of course they are right, but the 30 years is not meant to compensate. It is meant to rehabilitate and, secondarily, to warn other violence-prone individuals. If we cannot rehabilitate most human beings in 30 years, we are a society very deficient in wisdom about the human condition. I'd go a step further and say that the deficiency is in spiritual understanding, which includes the concept of redemption. It's not just an outmoded religious word.

Anger makes real spiritual development virtually impossible. I mean the lifelong growth of understanding our place in the universe. One reason I've never been interested in joining any traditional religious group is the emphasis on a package of beliefs assembled in the past, rather than on spiritual growth. Anger also looks backward, not forward. It's hard to develop while walking backwards.

The best training I've had in dealing with anger and establishing the conditions for growth is learning how to be present. It goes by other names such as mindfulness or awareness, and it is part of all the old wisdom traditions. It's essentially a spiritual practice, and it's very simple. You need to make a habit of noticing what is going on in you right now, from physical feelings to thoughts and emotions, without judgment. When you can do that you become, quite surprisingly, released from old stories, old tape recordings, and outdated instructions on how to be. You don't react to other people the way you used to react. You behave in a way appropriate to the present. It is very powerful.

There's one exception. One situation when anger is fully justified, appropriate, and, yes, honorable. That's when some maniac drives behind me at 75 miles per hour with one or two car lengths between us. Where did he learn to drive? Watching NASCAR races on TV? As a matter of fact, he is often a she these days, which further supports a point I made earlier about gender differences. I can't see any spiritual approach to this assault on my safety and well-being. Words fail me.

Life is sometimes fair, sometimes not. That's not a very profound way to conclude this rambling piece, but it's good to keep in mind. It needs to be woven into our beliefs and values as we go about becoming aware of our anger and developing our spiritual understanding. And that is done through self-education, insight, being present and, I suppose, growing older.

May you experience countless joys... and safe driving.

Love, Dad

The Comic Book Standard

For several years I participated in a men's discussion group. Over time we chewed over many issues in our lives. Relationships with women and children, medical problems, dissatisfaction with jobs and bosses, even sexual problems. In all that time, the one thing we never spoke of was our incomes. That was far too intimate.

Now I want to put down some thoughts on handling money, but no numbers, of course, because I still subscribe to the prohibition. Maybe we're afraid a tax man might be listening. Or someone needing a donation. Since one of my purposes in writing personal essays is to pass along something about me to my children and grandchildren, it's time to talk money.

How you think about money depends on many things, not least your age. If you came of age in the 1930's, the great depression was inescapable. You only needed to see the bread lines and poverty about you, whether or not you were part of it. If you came of age in late 1990's America, you naturally were influenced by the fortunes being created by technology, the booming stock market, the stratospheric earnings of celebrities such as sports stars, and the availability of easy money in all directions.

I was born in 1935 in a family with modest but regular income, and it didn't take long to learn that I was very fortunate. Although money was clearly limited, I was embarrassed at my position relative to some of my friends in public elementary school. This feeling was reinforced when I saw handicapped persons begging for coins along the streets of downtown Chicago, and the crowded homes of other kids – often two or three room apartments. These early experiences have certainly colored my political and social views.

So, as progressive as my opinions are on the world around me, I have always been conservative about money. It simply wouldn't occur to me to accumulate sizable personal debt other than my home mortgage. I've always paid cash for cars from savings, and I pay my credit card bills in full each month. I've always tried to keep six months expenses in readily available savings, and I've saved money every year except in some unemployment periods. It's not hard from this account to guess my opinion on our government running up a huge financial deficit. Yes, I know that countries differ from families. But not that much.

This conservative way of financial life had drawbacks in good times, when I missed some opportunities to make more money, but it has given me some peace of mind. I've had my share of life problems, but money does not rank high. One exception was a difficult period of unemployment when I had to pay my son's college tuition with a credit card. There are always exceptions.

I learned early that handling money is making choices. When I was a young boy, I developed a comic-book standard. When I would accumulate some cash from an allowance or gifts from relatives or from raking leaves, I decided how to spend it by comparing how many comic books it would buy versus another choice. 25 cents would cover two books, leaving a nickel, or it would pay for a Saturday matinee and some popcorn. The choice was mine; I couldn't do both. Some might find this too restrictive, but I liked the freedom to make choices. My standard has changed over the years, but the thinking process is similar.

Conservatism can become obsessive. For me, this tendency was reinforced in graduate school. Doing a research thesis, I felt compelled to find absolutely every reference, in every language, about my subject, despite knowing what they would say. For a time, I behaved like a collector who travels long distances to flea markets just in case someone has the piece of purple glassware missing from a collection.

Fortunately for me and those around me, this tendency was quickly dispelled when I entered industrial research. The premium there was on being smart and practical, not complete. I wonder whether this dose of common sense would have been available if I had pursued an academic life.

As it turned out, I loosened up about completeness in almost every aspect of my life except keeping track of money. Every month I balance my spending and income. I keep track of where my cash goes. I have done this since 1958, so I have a record of the cost of things for nearly half a century that fits in about three file boxes. Since the coming of personal computers, I probably spend about five hours a month on this task, so it's not very time consuming. My rationale is that I can forecast an annual budget quite closely. I know how much money we have for optional things like vacation trips and major house projects. Then we can make informed choices. The other benefit is that we have no need to budget all the regular expenses. They usually add up to last year's totals plus an inflation factor.

Let me back up a moment. My father worked for his father in a small family business manufacturing paint and varnish in Chicago. I worked there briefly before deciding to go in a different direction. I never knew my grandfather much. He was not much of a family man, and he was in declining health when I was a teenager. My understanding of him comes mostly from stories I heard after his lifetime.

The story I remember best is how he kept the company operating during the depression. The paint plant was in an old section of Chicago called Little Sicily. Most of the employees walked to work, and many were related in family groups. When times were hardest, his policy was to keep someone from every family on the payroll. That created considerable good will in the neighborhood, which I heard much about in later years. I have always thought of that as a good use of money, and I sadly contrast that policy with the modern bottom-line method of doing business.

Money is a complex subject. My life experiences are different from those of my children. Nevertheless I recommend using some kind of comic-book standard in making choices. Have enough cash for emergencies. Live within a balanced budget. Keep basic records but put your time and energy elsewhere. There are always exceptions.

March 7, 2005
Mozart, Lebron, and the Rest of Us

The President of Harvard recently got some very bad press by thinking out loud about differences between men and women in the sciences. Whatever the merit of his remarks, his public-relations skills could certainly use some attention. This episode prompted the following thoughts on skills, natural and acquired, bell curves, music, and basketball.

My basic skills. I was born in reasonable health and economic circumstances to two smart parents, so it's no surprise that I was smart in the school sense. Elementary and secondary education were made for people like me, as progress and rewards were based on reading, writing, and arithmetic. If the culture had, instead, required that we be graded primarily in music, art, and gym, my history would be considerably different.

So I found the prevailing culture quite comfortable. In retrospect, too comfortable, as I found little reason to develop some other life skills. This continued at MIT for about eight years, where I had to work much harder at things I was good at, but I still scored well. Along the way, I started to pick up a few more skills such as leadership and teamwork, logical thinking, and some ability to express myself in writing. All this education got me into a satisfying career track. Yet, so much was left out.

There's always someone smarter. This was one of the first important lessons from my MIT years. Not only smarter, but more adept socially, faster, stronger, braver, or able to speak or write better. I also discovered there are people who are willing and able to work harder to achieve a goal. Regarding raw talent, I had one teacher who, it was said, had logarithmic coordinates on his eyeballs so that he could see technical relationships that nobody else could see. I knew a student from Cambridge University who sat in lectures and never took notes, yet absorbed all he needed while the rest of us filled notebooks, with no better results. I still marvel at such individual skills.

Bell curves and beyond. Most of our skills and personal characteristics, relative to the population around us, fit on normal distributions or bell curves. If an ability is measurable on a scale of 1 to 10, over 90% of us score, say, from 3 to 7. This seems to apply to how fast we can run, how quickly we can solve math problems, or how accurately we can draw a figure on a piece of paper. If we can combine our natural skill with an ability to study and work diligently, we can and do move somewhat higher on the curve. As the old joke goes, the way to get to Carnegie Hall is practice, practice, and practice.

Perhaps the most interesting part of skill distributions is the high end – those who start life as a natural 9 to 10. In my undergraduate years at MIT, we were often graded on the curve. Tests contained more material than most students could complete. A typical undergraduate course exam might have an average of 40 on a scale of 100. A score of 60 would usually merit an A. MIT was more interested in students who could score 90 on that exam than those who scored 30, which was still satisfactory. The high achievers were targeted for graduate work. Early on, it was humbling to score 45 on a test until you got used to it.

What about those few exceptionally skilled individuals who seem to be part of a different distribution than the rest of us? I listen to a lot of Mozart's music, particularly the piano concertos and sonatas. How did he burst out of the conventions of his time, or any time, to create such beautiful pieces? It wasn't a long life of diligent work, as he died at 35 and had to scramble mightily to make a living. Mozart himself, in a letter, said that full compositions would simply come to him while he was walking in a park or riding in a carriage. He then went home and wrote it all down while Constanza was fixing dinner. My guess is that he had a very strong intuitive sense in the 9-10 range by which he picked up musical ideas from the universe. It was his musical training that then allowed him to put them on paper. This might be called a complex skill, a combining of two or more natural skills.

Sensory differences. Most adults easily understand the human range of differences in sight, hearing, taste, and odor differentiation. Any of them can be improved a bit, but we are by and large stuck with the senses we are dealt. In my family, my first wife is a classical singer who also has a very discerning ear for foreign language, such that she can get along in a foreign-language country within days of entering it. In contrast, I have a terrible time hearing foreign words even if I can read them. Our daughter has her mother's ear and ability to adapt to foreign language. Our son cannot even make out words in many American dialects. Such are the vagaries of genetics.

In the same vein, I have always loved many types of music. I can play wind instruments from sheet music and have a good sense of rhythm, phrasing, and style. But I just can't zero in on pitch. Some years ago I tried to learn jazz improvisation on the alto saxophone. I found it very difficult to translate musical ideas in my head to my fingers. Then I spent a week at a jazz camp, and heard kids 30 years younger than me create exciting improvised solos. They were obviously naturals. I was not.

As long as I'm confessing my shortcomings, a few words on visual memory. I have a poor one. I love to hear my fellow writers paint a picture of a scene 20 or 30 years ago in words that make it come alive, but such things do not come to me easily or at all. In our writing group, I may use the fewest adjectives of anyone for that reason, and I am hopeless at describing a sunset. I would not be a competent prose writer. Instead, I tend to write essays of ideas like this one – where I am most comfortable – and dramatic scripts consisting entirely of dialogue.

Complex skills. It's rarely sufficient in the world to be accomplished at just one thing. To achieve most goals, we need to combine skills – some we are naturally good at, and some we have to learn and cultivate. Often that requires a teacher, mentor, or supervisor to point that out. I mentioned Mozart's complex skills above.

In Cleveland, we are fortunate to have a superb 20 year old basketball player, Lebron James, who may become the greatest player ever, even counting Michael Jordan. In his few short years, someone – perhaps his high school coach – must have taught him that greatness in his profession requires a combination of athletic skill, with which he is generously endowed, people skills, for which he is already widely admired by his peers, and a strong sense of team effort. Night after night, he spends the first quarter of every game pulling his teammates into the game in remarkable ways. Other professional players are equally gifted athletes, but few exhibit his sure sense of working together to make his team play their best. How much of this sense is natural or intuitive, and how much is learned is unclear, but it's a rare combination.

Technical skill, sensitivity to people, and a sense of the larger picture. That's an example of complex skill.

Psychic skills. Psychic or intuitive ability probably fits on a bell curve, too. Too often it is suppressed because of our modern society's distrust of it. It simply does not fit our widespread materialistic, physical-science way of understanding our world.

Susan and I have attended many workshops and readings featuring psychic people. In several cases we have seen this ability in action, and I have written about a few. I've tried my own hand at it, and perhaps I have moved from 5.5 to 5.6 on a scale of 10, not quite enough to go into the forecasting business.

One thing I have gained is some sensitivity to psychic ability and experiences of other people. When we present the subject, people often tell us about their paranormal experiences that they do not tell their close friends. Even from a small sampling, I know that it is a widespread skill.

I teach a small group of eighth graders in Sunday School. Last fall I gave them an exercise to see what attributes they could pick up about an unknown object in a brown paper bag. After clearing their minds through a bit of guided imagery, they focused on the bag and wrote down what they sensed. We then looked at all the descriptions. Most did poorly. Perhaps because it was near noon and they were hungry, some were sure the bag contained food. It actually contained a quartz clock housed in a red, wood carving in the shape of a Volkswagen: red, smooth, and curved. One 13 year old boy had written down exactly those three adjectives. Later, I talked with his mother. She said he frequently understood things which were unexpressed, and he had a personal meditation practice. He could easily be a natural 9!

Healers come from many traditions, and have different approaches based both on their natural skills and the tradition they have studied, such as Reiki. They can be roughly divided into energy, spiritual, or psychic healers. There is a wide range of effectiveness among individual healers. That fact makes it difficult to decide whom to rely on. Most legitimate healers do have a sixth or seventh sense that is much more developed than the average person's. One example is a natural ability to see colored auras about a patient, from which the healer draws conclusions about health or disease in various parts of the body. Another example is the ability to sense subtle energy emanating from different parts of the body. Such skills, when coupled with good training, can be a strong diagnostic tool. The point is that these unusual skills do exist, although the great majority of us cannot find them in our own experience.

Myers-Briggs Personality Types. Around 1990 Susan and I attended a workshop on the Myers-Briggs personality test. This widely used tool, based on insights of Karl Jung, suggests there are 16 basic types of healthy personalities. You determine your type by answering a series of questions such as whether you prefer to gain knowledge by stewing over a problem yourself or by listening to other people. In a class situation, after we gathered in small groups of similar personalities, we found the "types" to be remarkably predictive of our attitudes toward hypothetical problems assigned to us.

We came away from this valuable experience with a fresh way to see differences between ourselves and people with whom we interact, professionally, socially, or within family relationships. We find that we do less complaining about someone's *different* way of behaving, and are more accepting of the natural distribution of personality traits.

Although we might wish that other people behaved like ourselves, they usually don't. We live on bell curves of differences.

Is industriousness a distributed natural skill? Some people seem to have high energy for work, for self improvement, or for focusing on tasks. Others don't. Part of this does seem to be natural or genetic, and part a consequence of health, education, and family circumstances. We admire those who rise above handicaps and achieve success in the world through grit and determination. In fact, the most admired skill seems to be the ability of someone to move beyond the limitations of birth and circumstance.

This universal attitude about self improvement often drives us to correct our deficiencies or work on minor skills quite apart from our main activities in life. In truth, it is often more rewarding personally, and more fun, to develop a new skill than to continue, on automatic cruise, doing what we are already good at. This is the drive underlying many avocations and hobbies.

Conclusions. It is extremely rare for someone to function at the highest end of two or more skills that complement each other, forming a unique complex skill. As rare as Mozart or Lebron James. More common is the need to develop complementary skills to support your best one.

Since each of us will never be very good at most activities, we have to choose whether to drop them, accept being mediocre, or enjoy the struggle. If we start life as a 3 (1-10 scale, again), hard work may get us to a 5 or 6 and a third-place ribbon, well earned. As much satisfaction can come from modest achievement as from high achievement. It's also good to remember that there is always someone smarter around.

March, 2006
The Zone

If I could make one wish for every young person, it would be to experience what it's like to be in the zone early in life. The zone is that region of performance, in almost any activity, where you function beyond concerns about technique or other people's expectations. Where you know you are operating at a high level, the best you can do. Where you feel totally comfortable and competent and right. Your memory of being in the zone often lasts long after the activity is completed. It can lead to achievement in many other parts of your life. It is much more than simple pleasure. It makes you glad to be alive.

Nowadays we tend to applaud or praise any positive achievement by young people, from getting an A on a test to scoring a goal at soccer. When you are actually in the zone, no applause is necessary. You just know where you are.

Prominent examples of being in the zone are evident in professional sports. I think of Michael Jordan's basketball play over the years – sometimes – or Tiger Woods' golf play in major championships – sometimes. They know when they are in the zone and when they are not, and no sportswriter need point it out. It is a great pleasure to see them operate. Yet the same personal experience is available in countless other arenas, and certainly in basketball and golf at lower levels of play. A few examples.

One of the attractions of jazz is the possibility of being at a concert or night club when a soloist goes into the zone. I've listened to hundreds of jazz performances but have only been present a handful of times when a musician enters the zone, inventing and expressing new musical ideas on the spot. It's even better when he draws the rest of the players into musical dialogue.

Some years ago I played in baroque music ensembles, which are distantly related to modern jazz music in the value of improvisation. I experienced a minor-league version of the ensemble effect when the group would catch a musical idea and pass it around. The whole group would go into the zone for short periods. No one wanted to stop.

Personal encounters often present opportunities to enter the zone. A teacher and a student. A business negotiation. A new friend, or an old one. These can be memorable experiences when expectations and training are left behind and the individuals are wholly engaged in communicating. Encounters work best when the parties are totally present with each other, oblivious to personal agendas or to other concerns of the moment. In fact, that seems to be the *requirement* for any activity taking place in the zone.

Any craft or artistic pursuit can be pursued at a routine level or can be elevated to the zone. You start with some level of training, education, or practical experience. When these factors, important as they are, are left behind, you have an opportunity to enter the zone. Consider cooking, something most of us do frequently and mostly routinely. For a special occasion, however, you want a unique dish that tastes, smells, and looks good. You already know what to do. The difference is your total investment in the activity. The result – a perfect omelet.

I love to write creatively. Essays and play scripts. Sometimes I write to meet a deadline, sometimes to bring a memory to life. Most often the results are fair, with a journeyman quality. Now and then something special happens and my fingers keep typing away while time passes. When I finally look at the clock, I'm surprised. I needn't tell other writers how good that feels, as it doesn't happen very often. I've seen muddy ideas suddenly become clear. I've seen characters come alive and take over a dialogue scene as if I am just the channel. I've been in the zone. There's simply nothing like it.

So how do you get beyond mere technique? You have sufficient training or experience so that there is no question what to do or how to do it. Those are the dues you must pay. You free yourself from the expectations of yourself or others. You become totally present in the activity. You see yourself and the activity as one. Then, with a little luck, you may enter the zone.

February, 2007

Diversity

The widely praised documentary series "Seven Up", now on DVD, follows the lives of fourteen English children, seven years old in 1963, every seven years through 2005. The latest installment is called "49 Up" and a large number of viewers around the world, including me, hope it continues. The format is mainly personal interviews with some shots of work and family settings.

The original premise of Seven Up is the Jesuit maxim, "Give me a child until he is seven, and I will give you the man." The lives that unfold through the series only partially support that notion, as the individuals take some surprising turns. It is such a pleasure watching this series yourself that I wouldn't spoil it for anyone. I raise two questions in this short reflection: At what age do people form fixed ideas about other people who differ in skin color, ethnic background, or financial circumstances? And how do they form these ideas?

In my own experience and in watching children and grand-children grow, I've observed that seven year olds are still mostly blind to racial and ethnic differences, although they are starting to notice them. By age 12 or 13, a lot of social attitudes are fixed, many for a lifetime. The key sources of these attitudes are parents and other family members, school experiences, and the opinions of peers and slightly older kids. I think media influence is of lesser importance.

Kids tend to lead their parents in social acceptance of others, particularly if their mix of friends and acquaintances differs from their parents'. This was certainly the case in my childhood in a diverse, integrated urban neighborhood. I've written elsewhere about my twelve year old understanding that one of my parents was simply wrong about people of different religious background. I knew my friends; my parents did not.

However, where I had no independent basis for deciding about different people, it was natural to accept the wisdom of the older generations. As an example, when I was a boy in the 1940's, I spent several summer weeks near Milwaukee among people of mostly German ancestry. I remember hearing jokes and seeing cartoons with bathroom humor, which was much less prevalent in my urban neighborhood in Chicago. I understood this was an earthy brand of German humor. Of course, it was easy, even patriotic, to put down the Germans during that period because of the war.

Around 40 years later, I had some brief trips to Holland as a lecturer in a commercial course on industrial technology. The students, engineers and chemists from various companies, were from all over continental Europe. After a few beers one evening, I mentioned that I had grown up with the idea that bathroom humor was characteristically German. They all jumped on me. No, they said, that is "English humor." I guess nobody owns it.

One important consequence of living in as diverse a society as America is one's exposure to differences. Those growing up in cities and progressing through public education seem to be much easier with diversity than those who spent their formative years in more isolated environments. Again, I think the most important years are around 6 to 12. Regarding the diversity of society, it's eye-opening to see attitudes in other cultures.

Last fall Susan and I took a commercial tour around Great Britain with a group of Americans. One pleasant morning in Edinburgh we visited the historical sights in the center of the city. Our guide was a mid-aged man dressed in a kilt, grey woolen jacket, and all the trimmings. He was an experienced tour guide and provided considerable historical detail as we traveled around in our bus and made several stops. When he discussed periods of construction, he remarked that the work was often slow and inferior when Irish laborers were brought in to do the work. I expect he would modify his spiel if the tourists were Irish. But why did he assume Americans would accept such remarks? Putting down the Irish, once common in America, disappeared here long ago.

America is certainly no paradise of progressive social attitudes, although I think it is more progressive than older, more homogeneous societies. But consider racial and ethnic jokes. For the last few years, a couple of my internet associations have included a continual barrage of jokes, stories, photographs, and cartoons send by e-mail. Some are truly funny, some are poignant, and some are genuinely patriotic. Some of the photographs are remarkable. But a fairly large number of the communications are jokes at the expense of somebody else. The last few years, the majority target either redneck hillbillies or Mexican immigrants, and more recently, Muslims. It is interesting that hardly any target African Americans. Those that do, deal with slum culture more than race as such. That's some kind of progress.

The acceptance of diversity is a long, slow process. My distaste for jokes and remarks putting down different racial and ethnic groups clearly came from my urban upbringing in those key years of childhood, and a public education. The English experience of fourteen kids in "Seven Up", mostly from the London area, is similar in many respects. Some of them came from highly privileged backgrounds, others from a lower economic class that was well defined in 1964 England. Yet they mostly appear to have adapted to the modern diverse society they grew into.

I got over my 1940's opinion of Germans later in life. Others, like the Scottish tour guide and some of my internet buddies seem to hold on to a need to differentiate themselves from other kinds of people. I'm certain it is grounded in the critical period of 6 to 12 years old. The life stories in "Seven Up" and my own experience do not support the Jesuit Maxim.

WHIMSICAL

March, 1999
Charlie

DEAR ANN LANDERS: This is in response to "Left-Brained in South Carolina," who needed a solution for dealing with his scatterbrained wife.

Every incident he cited, from losing keys to leaving items in odd places, has been done by my husband. Whenever "Charlie" gets ready to leave home, he has to search for his keys, wallet, checkbook or all three. He is also a slob. Any item he touches will be spilled, dropped, torn, lost, misplaced or mangled. His study looks like a tornado hit it.

I am organized and neat and never misplace anything, but I am also bad-tempered, inflexible, demanding and a perfectionist. I hardly ever relax. Charlie is easy-going, laid back and not easily upset. Who really has it roughest at our house? – *Another Left Brain in Redondo Beach, Calif.*

DEAR LEFT BRAIN: I'd say it's a tie, but I'll bet your husband's blood pressure is lower than yours.

Creators Syndicate (3-18-99)

DEAR ANN LANDERS:

I don't have much trouble getting along with most people. I've learned that people come in different flavors, and that's probably a good thing. Lately, however, I've been thinking that my wife and I are like mixing chocolate and vinegar.

I'm on a research team that's been working out how to put a man on Jupiter in April, 2035. That part's fun, to tell the truth. The hard part is getting him back – in case he wants to come back, of course. That's my job. As you can imagine, it keeps me busy.

I do some of my work at home in a study in the corner of the basement. It's become kind of a big deal with my wife. She wants me to put everything away every night as if a neatness inspector is coming in the morning. I don't mind lining up my toothbrush and razor in the bathroom and folding my towel up nice and square before I go to work, but I think my office is out of bounds.

Lately I've gotten real tense about this office thing, and a bunch of things seemed to happen all at once. I knocked over an open bottle of liquid Maalox. I couldn't find a receipt for some Girl Scout cookies I bought last year that she needs to do our taxes. This morning I was looking for my wallet and I tripped over the vacuum cleaner cord, which she keeps plugged in all the time just in case it's needed. Anyway, my car keys flew out of my hand and went down a heating duct, so I had to take her car for an important meeting. It was not a good week.

She's a good woman and keeps a nice house, but I'm beginning to wonder about this business of mixing our flavors. Do you think it's time to change the recipe?

Charlie

November, 2003

A Few of My Favorite Things

When my time comes to move on, I will surely miss the personal relationships in my life and the memories connected with them. But I will also miss many of the smaller things that color my days. Here are a few.

1. *The music of Richard Rodgers.* My favorite composers are Rodgers, J.S. Bach, and Mozart, in no particular order. Whenever I attend a performance of *Oklahoma* or *The Sound of Music*, it's good that the house lights come down before the curtain rises, for I'm simply overwhelmed by the opening numbers. Curly singing *Oh what a Beautiful Mornin'* in a cornfield, or Maria flitting about an Alpine meadow in *The Sound of Music*. Not to forget those magical tunes Rodgers wrote with Lorenz Hart in the thirties, which have become part of our permanent heritage.

2. *Blueberries.* Breakfast, from late June until well into October, is a bowl of cereal with blueberries. I count the beginning and end of summer to be coincident with price changes for a pint of blueberries. I keep buying them for weeks after the end-of-summer price increase, even as the boxes get smaller, trying to postpone the loss of those warm days when I could just put on a T-shirt and shorts and keep the windows open.

3. *Sinking a thirty foot putt.* I often play golf by myself, so I don't get the instant congratulations from playing partners for a good shot. Rather, I indulge in a bit of fiction that if only I practiced, I

might be able to play a decent game. That's the beauty of golf – once in a while you can stroke one like the champions. For me, that is a rare occurrence, so it counts a lot.

4. *A good medical report.* My body deteriorates at about the same rate that others do. The reports of its downward progress no longer come from a friendly family doctor after a session of poking, listening, and peering into my ears and throat and other places, but from a computer printout. It arrives in the mail a week or two after the rather impersonal annual exam or in a report from a specialist's office. In some ways that's better, but I still would like to have a physician who really knows something about me. Nonetheless, it's nice when most the numbers fall in the "normal" range, with a substantial assist from modern pharmacology, of course.

5. *Touching someone with words.* I've done quite a bit of writing the last few years: essays, plays, sermons. Once in a while something I've written sparks a new thought or insight in someone. That's very gratifying. So is the occasional conversation where the same thing happens. That is probably why I've never been very interested in "writing for the drawer", as they used to say in the Soviet Union. I need to try out my words on someone else.

6. *Coming home after a trip.* I don't have an urge to travel much for the sake of travel. Some friends are very nourished by travel, while others do it more out of restlessness. I had a boss once who much preferred moving about the country to working in his office. I think it was the kinetic activity of traveling that charged him up; he was actively *doing* something. Although I can get up for a trip to a specific destination, I like the endings best, when I turn into my street and see my house, still there.

7. *Having a new idea.* This might be at the top of this list if I were ranking things. When I was 13, while trying to figure out what I thought about my religious training, I had a moment when I realized that I would have to think for myself. I remember exactly where I was, too. It seems appropriate in retrospect that I had a career in industrial research and development, where I was paid to think of new ways to put chemicals together or design a process or solve a problem. Because I worked in a narrow technical area, there were a few times that I was pretty sure that I was the only person in the world to have a certain new insight. Most of the time, of

course, the idea was new to me but not to the world. I treasure all those moments.

8. *Cryptic crossword puzzles.* I got hooked by this small subset of puzzles twenty years ago. The definitions are wrapped up with a clue you have to decipher. Most of the words are common, but the clues are intricate. The first two or three that you try require many hours to unravel. Perhaps it's that initial investment of time that does the hooking. Cryptics appear in the back of *Harper's* and the *Atlantic Monthly,* and elsewhere. I claim that there is nothing like a cryptic to keep the gears in our brain lubricated, but that may sound suspiciously like an addiction. Maybe it's genetic, as my father loved crossword puzzles.

9. *Chocolate chip cookies from Corky and Lenny's.* I've eaten chocolate chip cookies from hundreds of sources. Big, small, soft, hard, chewy, crunchy... These are the best.

10. *Naps.* A good night's sleep is too easy to take for granted, and it's not always so good if you have chronic sinus congestion as I do. But there is nothing like a good nap in a comfortable chair, preferably on a balmy summer afternoon, letting your mind drift a bit just before dozing off. Maybe remembering a tune. Let's see... How does that start? That's it... *The hills are alive with the sound of music...*

February, 2008
Ten More

In 2003, I wrote "A Few of My Favorite Things", ten small things that add color to my days. Enough time has passed to add ten more to the list. As before, I omit the more important markers of my life: personal relationships, big events, successes and failures. With a bit of luck, I'll do this again in 2013. Now, that's hubris.

1. *"Summertime"*. George Gershwin's beautiful song, a lullaby, is the favorite of many people, including me. It comes to life less than a minute into *Porgy and Bess* when a young mother carrying a baby strolls into the square of Catfish Row. How can one not shiver with excitement when the familiar opening notes sound in the bass, followed by her soaring high notes. *Summertime, when the livin' is easy...*

2. *Chocolate cheesecake.* No more than three or four times a year I have a slice of chocolate cheesecake. Although infrequent, these occasions are much anticipated. The question is always whether the product is worth the wait. Too often it is not, lacking either the perfect creamy texture or the right amount and type of chocolate. I have two models of excellence stored in my taste buds, or wherever such things reside. One is a dessert at an Italian restaurant in Mayville, NY in 2006. The other, a homemade version, appears on the shelf at a local market once in a while. I suppose other factors enter the equation, such as my mood, the quality of the preceding meal, the weather, sun spots, whatever. But such things influence other judgments, too.

3. *Children playing.* Is there a sound more joyful to the ear than young children playing outdoors on a summer day? Whether they are throwing a ball around or playing hide and seek, their focus is total, as is their immediate pleasure. You hope it can last forever but you know better. Still, if I were a composer, I would try to capture that music.

4. *Human interest stories.* Nationally syndicated and local columnists are worth reading most days. So are the comics and the daily accounts of our professional athletes. But one reason I read my local paper every day is the human interest story, often featured on page one. Heroic teenagers, the reuniting of long-lost relatives, struggles to rise above poverty or loss, lives devoted to service and caring, many obituaries. I also am drawn to the short statements of gratitude published once a week about people helping snowbound elders, or the return of a lost wallet, or house visits at times of need. Young people who don't bother with a daily paper miss these; it's a loss.

5. *Military music.* When I was in the peacetime Army, I enjoyed marching in formation to John Philip Sousa's music, and later, leading a company in marching past a reviewing officer. I still like to hear the music and tap my foot. Perhaps it's the invigorating sense of being part of a group acting as one. Of course, that's the point of it all, militarily. Get ready. A whistle blows. *The Stars and Stripes Forever* starts. Let's go!

6. *Flirting.* I guess that's the right word. I'm thinking about brief unexpected encounters with someone of the opposite sex, if you are oriented that way, where you both sense a mutual attraction. Then it's done with, although it can linger in memory for some time. I find it life-affirming, although that may be too fancy a term. It doesn't happen often, as most of us carry a fairly efficient protective shield around our feelings, for both good and bad reasons. Maybe it's similar to meeting a good slice of chocolate cheesecake.

7. *Tap dancing.* I'm part of that subset of the world population that loves good tap dancing. A few years ago someone sent me an internet link to a long sequence of Fred Astaire and Eleanor Powell dancing in *Broadway Melody* of 1940. When I run into another tap enthusiast, I soon send him or her that clip. Also a few years ago, I

bought some size 13 tap shoes and enrolled in a couple of classes of mostly young women. The classes were discontinued; it was just as well, as I was a bit slow. Besides, I was not in tune with the contemporary music used for instruction. But I can still picture myself as Fred Astaire.

8. *Adding columns of numbers.* This skill has rapidly disappeared since the invention of handheld calculators. Yet I find an occasional person of my age who admits to the pure pleasure of zipping down, then up, a column of numbers and writing the sum down without electronic assistance. It is rarely useful anymore, perhaps for quickly checking a bridge score after an evening of duplicate play, or a golf score on the run. It dates back to elementary school when we also diagrammed sentences and filled ink wells.

9. *Wooden pencils.* My long-standing favorite is a Ticonderoga No. 3, yellow with a red eraser, and a metallic green band holding the eraser. There are a couple sitting next to my computer right now – for making notes. I like to sharpen them too, catching the odor of freshly shaved cedar. Wooden pencils are hard to find. These were on the lowest shelf at an OfficeMax under hundreds of pens and markers of all types. They are good for adding columns of numbers, by the way.

10. *Spring.* By far, my favorite season is Spring, despite the onset of special sinus problems and an occasional reversion to winter for a couple of days to keep us honest. Crocuses, daffodils, flowering trees. Put away winter coats. Replace storms with screens. Start the golf season. Renewal and restarting, those are the motifs. The very best thing about Spring is the promise that Summer is coming... *Summertime, when the livin' is easy.*

POLITICAL

March, 2002

Foreign Policy: A Grandfather's View

We hear often that our world has changed. It did change in August, 1945, when we twice demonstrated that technology can be used to kill huge numbers of people in less time than it takes to write this. In the postwar years an American consensus grew: three ideas that guided our foreign policy.

1. We can never again use weapons of mass destruction. We continued to develop them defensively so they would never be used.

2. If our country or its vital interests were attacked, we would use conventional military power in measured reprisal.

3. We must continually strive for international cooperation, more equitable sharing of earth's resources, and the gradual reduction of national and other barriers between peoples.

Many good things resulted from this consensus. The rebuilding of Europe and Japan. The United Nations. Free trade policies. Containment of the USSR's imperial ambitions. A nonmilitary resolution of the cold war. Fifty years of exporting American graduate education. Cooperation in space. The internet. There's a list of bad things too, most often when point 3 was disregarded for short-term reasons, political or economic.

Recent actions in Washington threaten to undermine all three points. Has the consensus changed? I don't think so.

Since 9/11, letters to editors, TV and internet commentary, published columns and essays have contained many thoughtful statements from all parts of our population. Although there are some reasoned arguments for military action, the great majority of commentators find the international situation considerably more complex, calling for more complex initiatives. This continuing dialogue, not mindless flag waving, represents the popular consensus. It is poorly represented among the political leadership of both parties.

In dealing with international conflicts, the alternative to military action is diplomacy. How is it going? Senior administration officials are currently making the rounds of Middle Eastern countries. From all accounts, they appear to be looking for support of military action in Iraq rather than nonmilitary solutions. This is not diplomacy and it is not consistent with our popular consensus.

The current world scene cries out for active diplomacy. Why are we not sending one mission after another to the Middle East to search for common ground? There is always common ground, as simple as a better life for the people involved. We seem willing (sometimes) to mediate disputes involving other nations, but what about our own interests and disputes? What does Iraq want, and what do we want? Those simple questions are the basis for diplomacy, or for negotiation at any level.

I sense distrust, possibly fear of diplomacy in Washington. Why? Maybe we are not very good at it. Maybe it is too slow a process that can't be concluded in a month, a year, or an election cycle. It may have to do with the kind of people we put in power.

In national elections of my time, most of the candidates and their close advisors have been energetic, highly competitive, and smart. These qualities are sufficient and necessary for getting elected, but insufficient for governing this country. What is needed is a good dose of wisdom based on public experience and understanding of our cultural values and history, along with a high standard of ethics. Too often we get energy at the expense of wisdom.

Perhaps the most interesting historical question of the last 50 years is how we have avoided a nuclear war. In a recent column, Ellen Goodman called it "something of a miracle." Reading accounts of the Cuban missile crisis and other cold war episodes, one can only shudder at how close we came. In contrast, the USSR was headed by a politburo that appeared to be mostly grandfathers. One trait of grandparents is their extreme reluctance to start throwing nuclear warheads around. I don't know a better explanation.

Somehow military power has been elevated to the top of the list in our dealings with the world. It does not represent the popular consensus that has served us well. I have to conclude that our system of electing people to national leadership is deficient in that it selects competitive warriors over skilled negotiators, action over reflection.

Perhaps we need more grandparents in Washington.

March, 2003
The Welfare of the Troops

When I was trained for peacetime Army duty, one of the lasting lessons I got in ROTC was the doctrine that a military commander always had at least two basic responsibilities: the mission and the welfare of the troops. There was no single bottom line, always two, and more at higher levels of command.

If more of our business and political leaders had been taught this simple directive early in their careers, our public life would be different, and better.

In business, we have seen the results of bottom-line thinking. The most widely followed mission in corporations today is to maximize this quarter's profits. Incentive systems that guide executives reinforce this mission by rewarding the leadership with stock options that make reported earnings the only measure of success. Earnings growth leads to stock value growth, in turn to handsome personal fortunes for those holding options.

Yet, corporations get their charters from governments, which offer certain financial protection in return for creating economic growth and opportunity within society. A corporation has several constituencies or stakeholders: employees, managers, stockholders, customers, suppliers, communities, government bodies, and the environment. All these stakeholders include both present and future components. An emphasis on the bottom line essentially disregards all but today's stockholders and top executives.

We have seen the economic chaos and human cost that result from this way of running big business in the spectacular rise and fall of far too many companies. In contrast, privately held companies, where the owner's children stay in the business, often are run to ensure long-term health.

In politics, the principal goal appears to be getting re-elected instead of governing. Political decisions are made to satisfy those individuals and groups who contribute money or swing votes for the next election. Money, of course, buys TV advertising and internet communication, which are widely understood to win elections.

If we look at the nature of debate in our Federal government, we see too little discussion of the merits of opposing views on policy, and too much attention paid to what will affect the next election. As a result, the lower economic levels of our population, who do not contribute to political campaigns and rarely vote, get just enough to keep them from revolting, while the financial supporters of both parties get well treated.

The deterioration of big business and big politics in a democratic society can be halted by changes in incentives – by a restructuring of the system. We might start by teaching our future leaders about stakeholders and the need to balance multiple responsibilities in public life. It's a simple lesson, really. One that made sense to a 20 year old ROTC student some time ago.

October, 2004

Marketing Ourselves Out of Iraq

Published in the Cleveland Plain Dealer as an Op-Ed Column,
titled "Give Iraqis Credit Cards and Catalogs"

The numbers are hard to grasp. We have either spent $120 billion or $200 billion on the Iraq invasion so far, depending on which candidate you believe. Whatever figure you accept will likely double in the next few years under present policy. By any measure, this is an excessive cost for settling Western-style democratic capitalism on an Islamic country of 25 million people.

Taking a conservative view, let's assume that the total monetary cost, by the time this is over, is $250 billion. That comes to $10,000 per Iraqi, or perhaps $25,000 per Iraqi family. These figures suggest a plan to end the war.

Why not issue credit cards worth $10,000 to every Iraqi, just quit fighting and call it a win? Let's require that half the money must be used for purchases from America. That means that what we have spent so far would quickly come back to the US in retail purchases as a sorely needed stimulus to our economy. The other half, spent elsewhere, would serve to dampen criticism in the rest of the developed world. As a bonus, the cash would be a good start in building a capitalist culture, thus furthering the objective of our invasion.

To be competitive, our retailers would have to translate catalogs into Arabic and expand their offerings to include merchandise that meets the need of Iraqis; these efforts would greatly increase our country's knowledge of that culture. Every day, when I receive two or three fall catalogs in the mail, I reflect on how hard it is to sell things to a population that is pretty well stocked up on designer jeans and monogrammed bar glasses. What an opportunity for creative marketing! In the retail business, $125 billion is real money.

Of course there would be problems. One that comes to mind immediately is the charge of unfairness that would arise in the rest of the world and even in parts of this country. In a short time, 10 or 20 countries would ask to be invaded. Some would offer better deals than others, creating further opportunities. Mexico, for instance, might suggest that its citizens would stop crossing the border to work. Although Southwestern states would resist this loss of cheap labor, we could counter by offering relocation allowances to returning National Guard soldiers who could replace the Mexican workers.

The other big problem is what to do when the credit cards are used up. Strategic planning is the answer to both problems. We simply announce our intention to invade a new country, or the same old countries, about once a year. After the obligatory speeches about spreading democracy, we sit down and negotiate a new credit card deal. Thus the beginnings of a 21st century foreign policy.

I'm ready to donate a three foot stack of recent catalogs to help get it started. Where do I send them?

May, 2006

Estes Kefauver Remembered

I spent the spring and summer of 1960 in Oak Ridge, Tennessee, as part of my graduate school program. The town was changing rapidly, as the security fences surrounding it since 1943 had recently been taken down. Only the three atomic energy installations were still carefully guarded, as I'm sure they remain today. The state of Tennessee, along with the rest of the country, was also caught up in major change, the civil rights revolution.

1960 was also an election year. Senator Estes Kefauver was running for reelection to a seat he had held since 1948. In his first twelve years in the Senate he became known as a strong advocate of consumer protection and civil liberties. He chaired the Senate Crime Investigating Committee and the Antitrust and Monopoly Subcommittee. In 1954 he was the only Senator to vote against a measure making it a crime to belong to the Communist Party. In 1956 he was the Vice Presidential candidate with Adlai Stevenson, a ticket that lost in the second Eisenhower landslide.

What I most remember about Kefauver that summer was the stump speech he gave over and over throughout Tennessee. He told his listeners that his conscience simply prohibited him from denying civil rights to black Americans. He was often called too liberal for Tennessee. On election day, nobody could be found who would admit voting for him. Yet, when the returns were counted, he won with nearly 65% of the vote. The people clearly had listened, and had spoken.

We seem to have lost this kind of national politician in an era of sound bites and issue manipulation. A consistent, well-grounded person who knows what he or she believes and lets people know it up front. With Kefauver in mind, I'm looking for a presidential candidate who starts by making clear what he or she really believes about the so-called morality issues. These are the issues that have been injected into modern campaigns solely to draw votes from targeted groups. Abortion, gay rights, flag burning, religious piety, and racism in its many forms.

Now, as then, I hope the candidate would say "Now it's time to talk about the real political issues that I would address when in office." National problems such as the use of military power, budget imbalance, health care, energy, and education.

We badly need another Kefauver. I believe the country would respond as Tennessee did 46 years ago. I would not be surprised if he or she could win over 60% of the popular vote. In fact, I'd bet on it.

Made in the USA
Charleston, SC
14 January 2010